Beyond the Behavior Contract

Other Books by Brett J. Novick

Parents and Teachers Working Together: Addressing School's Most Vital Stakeholders

The Balanced Child: Teaching Children and Students the Gifts of Social Skills

The Likable, Effective, and Productive Educator: Being the Best You Can Be as an Educator

Beyond the Behavior Contract

A Practical Approach to Dealing with Challenging Student Behaviors

Brett J. Novick

ROWMAN & LITTLEFIELD
Lanham • Boulder • New York • London

Published by Rowman & Littlefield
An imprint of The Rowman & Littlefield Publishing Group, Inc.
4501 Forbes Boulevard, Suite 200, Lanham, Maryland 20706
www.rowman.com

6 Tinworth Street, London SE11 5AL, United Kingdom

British Library Cataloguing in Publication Information Available

Library of Congress Cataloging-in-Publication Data Is Available

978-1-4758-4389-7 (cloth: alk. paper)
978-1-4758-4393-4 (pbk: alk. paper)
978-1-4758-4394-1 (electronic)

I would like to dedicate this book to my late father, Dr. William A. Novick, who taught me how to be a father. To my parents, who taught me the importance of hard work and values. My wife, Darla, who teaches me each and every day how to be a better and happier person, parent, educator, and spouse. My children, Billy and Samantha, who give me hope for a future generation with pride.

Thank you to Tiffany Aguayo for being my informal editor in this book. Also, to the many other professionals and students whom I have had the honor of working with over the years who have taught me so very much. Please know, it has been an honor to be allowed to play a small part in your lives. To the many mentors who, in both education and life, inspired me in every aspect of my life. Thank you.

Contents

Preface

Let us remember: One book, one pen, one child, and one teacher can change the world.

—Malala Yousafzai

Have you noticed student behavior seemingly worsening over the past several years? The conversation has, no doubt, become the topic of heated dialogue in the faculty rooms of schools across our nation and spilled over to the dinner tables of homes from sea to shining sea. Some naysayers might dispel these discussions with the skepticism of the elder professional that state, "That is because back in the good ole' days kids respected their teachers!"

So the question remains: Are children's negative behaviors really escalating? Or, in turn, is it just the imagination of educational professionals who are burnt out from a deluge of seemingly endless standardized testing, core curriculum standards, and devaluation of the teaching profession as a whole?

No, it is not your imagination regarding the sharp rise in pupil misbehavior. In a recent report entitled *Primary Sources: America's Teachers on the Teaching Profession*, which was conducted by Scholastic and Bill & Melinda Gates Foundation, increased behavioral problems have been seen across grade levels: 68 percent of elementary school, 64 percent of middle school, and 53 percent of high school teachers. Among veteran teachers (who have been in the same school for more than five years), 62 percent of this population indicate a significant worsening of pupil behaviors within their classes.[1]

Further, turning on our televisions at night over the past two decades, we have borne witness to what happens when a *perfect storm* of mental illness, rage, and evil lies claim to the lives of innocent children and educators. Often, it results in a spike in a quagmire of discussing guns, mental illness, religion, and politics. What happens at the end of the day? It stalls at the end of the day under the heat and complexity of an issue with no easy answers.

There are a host of reasons as to why such misbehaviors may be escalating and are in desperate need of examination. They have proven to be a source of hotly contested debate as to which of these facets is more of a factor than another. There are a host of experts and laypersons who say, "Try this or try that," various theories and speculations as to what to do with behavior challenges in the classroom.

The question still remains: What do you do when you have a child "flipping out" and tearing up a classroom? The answers are all too easy when one is playing armchair quarterback and suggesting strategies from the sidelines. The fact is there is no one-size-fits-all strategy for every child. We are constantly tailoring academics around the way a child learns, and so we must also sculpt our interventional techniques to the way a child behaves, thinks, and functions.

Of course, resistance can be met along the way. People will say things like, "That child should know better!" "You must give respect to get respect!" "In the real world, they will not accept [fill in the blank]!" These statements are said under one's breath or, more often, said aloud in the utterance of frustrations that we all feel as educators.

More and more, educators are expected to pick up the pieces of parenting that society anticipates are increasingly in the domain of public education. At the same time, educators are under assault politically and are provided less and less in terms of support, to help bolster their needs with these ever more challenging children.

In our time together, I hope to offer you some assistance in this matter. Please let me be clear, unless you are in the classroom with the particular challenging student who sits in front of you, no one can know the challenge that lies before you, to teach not only academics but also life skills, social skills, appropriate emotional expression, and social work. These are the hats that you must simultaneously don each and every day. Education is now a job of many roles intertwined into a single person.

Before we start, thank you for all of your hard work in teaching and sculpting our next generation. Remember that it is from your never-ending dedication that creates the roots from which all children grow and bloom. You have the key to the future in your hands—a tremendous burden and responsibility.

NOTE

1. Scholastic, *Primary Sources*, Third Edition, www.scholastic.com/primary sources/.

Introduction

Human behavior flows from three main sources: desire, emotion, and knowledge.

—Plato

Under the bright fluorescent lights and the worn-out 1970s-style orange-and-brown couches of the faculty room of the Anytown School System in Anywhere, the United States, a conversation is going on right now as you read this book.

The conversation, though seemingly casual and subtle, is about the very future of our world. It is a casual conversation replicated thousands of times, in hundreds of thousands of schools. It's an interaction about how we can navigate children's behavior and social skills back onto "the tracks" of social norms within our school and, indeed, the future world that awaits them.

It is a conversation that determines whether children will succeed in a world that requires them to take responsibility for themselves as adults or, alternatively, fail in an environment that they deem as fostering anger, hostility, and injustice at every turn.

That very conversation goes something like this:

Teacher #1: "That kid in my class is unbelievable! He does whatever he wants, whenever he wants to. When I tell him he can't do something, he doesn't listen. In fact, he does the exact opposite!"

Teacher #2: "Did you try a behavior chart? I have one in my class where the kids work to earn extra time on the computers. They like that!"

Teacher #1: (Sighs) "He doesn't seem to care about anything like that. All's that he tells me is that he doesn't care about this or that. He is exhausting and takes up the whole classes' time and frustrates me."

Teacher #2: "Did you call his parents?"

Teacher #1: "Yeah, they are of no help. They say that is just the way he is. Then they told me he is even worse at home! I can't even imagine that!"

Teacher #2: "Did you tell Mr. Jones [the principal]?"

Teacher #1: "He doesn't care even if Mr. Jones visits my class. For him, it is like a break!"

Teacher #2: "Wow, I am sorry. I am all out of ideas. It is going to be a looonnggg school year for you."

Teacher #1: "Yeah, I hope I even make it through the year!" (Tears well up in her eyes.)

Variations of this conversation go on each day, of each academic year. They are frustrating because they often end with a burnt-out teacher who has more questions than answers. They leave that teacher seeking and hoping that something will work—a "magic pill" or intervention that will immediately solve the behavioral issue and quell the unrest that bubbles up within the classroom.

Just to be clear, unfortunately, there is no such "magic cure." However, there are many practical tools that you can apply immediately. Some will work better than others depending on the varying students you work with.

Some of our children struggle with reading, math, and coordination in physical education classes and (yet others) struggle with behavior. This turmoil may be due to a number of physiological, environmental, parental, and socioeconomic factors. We will never know to what degree each of these impacts our children.

What we do know is just as we tailor academics to each of our students, so must we tailor approaches to these pupils. We must teach to their strengths (which may not be social skills, behavior, emotional expression, self-esteem, or anger management). From this we can see the proverbial "forest for the trees." We must constantly remind ourselves that we seek steady progress and will not achieve behavioral perfection.

In our world none of us reaches the lofty goal of doing everything right, handling every situation with care and tact, or not losing our temper once in a while. As the educator, however, you have a unique and vital opportunity to be the one who shapes these children toward success and dealing with life's failures.

As an educator you will teach how to succeed as a student as well as a member of society. Speaking of society, it takes a system (aka "village") to raise a child. It is not the parent, the teacher, the coach, the specific classroom intervention, or the student. Ideally, it is all of those together making a synergistic change.

All of those coming tougher optimally is a "pie in the sky" philosophy, and we all know that we generally do not get all of those pieces with any child. Many of these children have had the pieces of life shattered, and the puzzle may not be able to complete in its entirety again. That being said, however, we can tweak parts of all these to make a significant transformation in the lives of many of our youth.

Chapter 1

The Home

Understanding Behavior from the Context of the Home

Knowledge is power. Information is liberating. Education is the premise of progress, in every society, in every family.

—Kofi Annan

Michael bounds up the crumbling cement stairs to his home and leaps over the rusted coffee can that is filled to the brim with discarded cigarette butts. He puts his hand through the torn screen door and opens the secondary white door that is weathered and splintered.

As he opens the door to his house, he looks at the mosaic of spills and stains that lie upon the carpets. On a table lies the discarded food from a few days ago that seems to be in constant motion with the flies that hover around the once-eaten morsels.

He searches his home for an area to put his books down. That is not easy, because the house is piled up with papers, old containers of every shape and size, and a menagerie of every imaginable item. The inside of his house looks more akin to a landfill than a home, but this is what he is used to; this is his "normal."

This week the power is on, but there is no water in the house. Every week or so one utility is off. So, this week they have to go to the neighbor's home to shower or to use the restroom. Last week, he was doing his homework by flashlight, but it was hard because he was wearing three sweaters, necessary to warm himself as his mother mentioned something about having no heat "because it was electric."

Speaking of his mother she is nowhere to be found today. He looks for her and is not certain if she was trying to go to another doctor to get more pain medicine for her "back" or at work overnight. Not a note left to explain her whereabouts. Either way, he knows one thing: he is alone and probably will be for the rest of the night.

His mother always warns him when he is by himself to lock the doors to the house. He knows this is a good idea because he has seen people selling drugs outside at the park across the street. He also sees the gangs are always looking for young, new members and has seen what happens when the old members try to leave.

She tells him "he is the man of the house," since his dad finally left after beating up his mom. (That was not a new thing. He used to do this since Michael was a baby.) It worries him being "man of the house"; he is small and not strong enough to be "a man." He lets his mind wander and thinks if he learns karate or maybe carries a knife, he can protect his mom and his family.

Michael checks, for the third time, that the door is locked and begins trying to do his homework. His thoughts drift off: "Where could my mother be? Wait! What was that noise outside? What should I do? Play a video game instead of doing homework?"

He decides that playing on his tablet is easier than doing his homework; with no one to supervise him, he goes and plays with his tablet until 2 a.m. Eventually, he drifts off into a fitful sleep by the dull glow of his tablet.

WHAT CHILDREN CONTROL AND WHAT THEY DON'T

Imagine that you get aboard a plane during a stormy night. Your knuckles are white as you grip the armrest in fear that the plane may crash. Then, the pilot comes on the intercom, "Hi folks, this is Captain Smith from the flight deck. I anticipate a smooth flight to California. Just sit back, relax, and enjoy the flight."

The careful, calm, and strong voice of the pilot is reassuring. You think to yourself, surely he knows what he is doing and he is prepared for any issue should it arise and you are going to get to California in one piece. You close your eyes and sink back into your seat, feeling calm and assured that everything is okay.

Now, let's look at a parallel scenario. You get aboard that same plane during that identical stormy night. Your knuckles are as white as before, and you are just as afraid of that plane going down in a fiery streak of debris. Now, the pilot comes on the intercom, "Hi folks . . . this is [an audible pause] . . . Captain Jones from the flight deck." You notice a distinct tone of distress and worry in his voice. "We are flying to New York . . . and no worries, I have over 10,000 flight hours . . . in the simulator. No worries though [he chuckles nervously], this is my first cross-country flight."

Now, how do you react? Instead of sinking back into your seat, you feel a pit in the core of your stomach, your heart races, and your stomach is suddenly queasier than before. Your eyes dart back and forth looking for any subtle changes or noises throughout the flight as the hair stands up on the back of your neck.

Think of parents as those pilots and their children as their passengers. Depending on how competent those parents "pilots" are to their families will mean the difference between passengers who feel comfortable, safe, and validated and those who are out of control and seeking to find a parachute at the first mention or sound of potential trouble.

An additional thought: If you are the pilot of your classroom, is your class flying smoothly like Captain Jones or more akin to the turbulent Captain Smith? Do your students feel that you are in control and the routine is predictable, or do they feel that they are in the back of a wild and chaotic ride of volatility? That is the question.

Children, in fact, have very little control over anything in the world. Think about what items they can control. The majority of their lives are under the Marshall Law of adulthood.

Here are what children can control, and do so, with a stubborn steadfastness:

What I am going to eat: If you look at what most children prefer to eat, it is pizza, hot dogs, chicken nuggets, and mac and cheese. Why? Because they know they can exert control over what goes into their mouths and they can also close their mouths and avoid eating what you give them. Case in point, watch a toddler spray food out of his or her mouth in protest.

When I am going to sleep: Often parents have difficulty getting their children to sleep. The youth procrastinates, asks for a drink of water, and/or wants to go to the bathroom for the twelfth time. Conversely, as they get older, that struggle changes to not wanting to get up in the morning.

What I am going to wear: Girls are especially keen in using this tactic. Children may tell you what they are going to wear or not wear. They cannot be forced to wear something they don't want to wear.

When I am going to use the bathroom: Children even use the bathroom as a matter of control. Some children hold their bladders or bowels to a point of becoming ill, if their world is out of control. Or, they may choose to urinate or soil themselves to show that they can control some element of their lives (no matter how small). Not sure if a child uses toileting as a matter of control? Think about this, when you go out to dinner and you ask your child, "Do you need to use the bathroom *before* the food gets here?" the answer is usually a resounding "No!" When the hot meal that smells delectable gets there, the child suddenly has to use the bathroom "urgently." Is it due to some connection between smell and toileting? Not likely; it is the child's perceived ability to control an adult from getting to do what he or she is most looking forward to doing and channel it into further attention for the child.

BOUNDARIES AKA "SHOULD THEY KNOW NOT TO DO THAT?"

Where did you learn what you were supposed to do and not supposed to do? Where did you acquire your social skills? Conflict resolution skills? Life skills? Most of us learned these, at some point, from our parents and/or those adults who were close to us and taught us via example and direction.

Keep in mind, if you are not given these examples, you must learn the hard way. In short, you simply don't know what you don't know. If no one told you the rules of the game of life, how well would you fare? If no one modeled how to be a productive member of society, how do you learn?

Now, I am not saying that every child having behavioral issues has parents who do not teach them. What I am saying is don't *assume* that every child knows, or understands, boundaries the way that you expect they should. Just as you don't assume that a child has knowledge of your curriculum previous to his or her entering the classroom setting.

YOU CAN ONLY BE AS HEALTHY A FISH AS THE WATER YOU SWIM IN

As an avid aquarist, I have had many fish tanks and different types of fish—saltwater, tropical, freshwater, outdoor, and indoor. I have had them all. Each has different requirements, supplements you must aid, and temperatures that you must maintain in the tank.

Yet, the one element they all have in common? The quality of the water. Without proper water quality all fish eventually become sickened no matter how strong they are or the size of the tank they reside.

So, it is with children. As an educator, you work with children six hours per day if you are lucky. Then they are left to go back to the same environment for the other eighteen hours. It can seem futile that you spend six hours teaching, counseling, and working with the children only to turn them back into the tumultuous, murky waters of a difficult family.

Remember one thing, however, you can look at it as though what is the use of the six hours of hard work when you will have it unwoven over the next eighteen, or so, hours. Or you can look at it that you have given the child a few breaths of fresh air, someone who believes in them, and hope in those precious six hours. The students who are most misbehaving are the ones who are also most craving of that very attention, consistency/structure, and safety.

THE CONSISTENCY OF INCONSISTENCY AND HOW IT WORKS AGAINST YOU IN THE CLASS

If you have ever had the opportunity to go to a casino, you will see the potent strength of inconsistent reinforcement at its best. Watch those glazed-over eyes of people of all ages playing the slot machines. It is as if some zombie-like trance has taken them over and they continue to pour coins in and perform the simple task of pulling the lever hypnotically.

This ritual goes on hour after hour every day as bells ring and echo throughout the entire casino. Simulated sounds of coins pouring out are heard in albeit less but regular tones on the casino floor. So how does this show inconsistency in a classroom?

Well, first let's go back to those glazed-eyed individuals who are pumping potentially hundreds of dollars per hour into a machine. Judging from the gold-trimmed palace of the casino around them, they are not earning money anytime fast. In fact, they are losing hundreds but are reinforced with paltry amounts: sometimes thirty or forty dollars (versus the hundreds or thousands they are losing).

So why would anyone do this? Why would you "donate" thousands to a casino, only to get back maybe a hundred or two and, rather illogically, consider yourself "lucky"? Well, psychologically, that inconsistent reinforcement unconsciously teaches you that you must work harder (not smarter) to get some payout. Perhaps that next pull, that next try, will have you living on easy street and getting the "big payout" of what you want.

Now, let's shift back to that child at home. If a parent is being *consistently* inconsistent, what happens is a child pulling on the proverbial (and maybe actual) arm of that parent like that slot machine. Each time the child tries it may mean that he or she has a slight chance of getting what he or she wants in the form of a "payout." Often, in the psyche of the child it ultimately works at some point, so keep trying. Try the third time, the first time, or the tenth time, and you get what you want. If not? The child is simply not working hard enough or with the right strategy.

Then the child comes to school. The teacher sets consistent rules and expectations. Yet, it takes a significant amount of time for that child to recognize that he or she is not going to win in this parallel behavioral gamble at school. The child may try to get around it, over it, under it, or wear you down and go through it. All of this is done until the child knows that he or she *absolutely* cannot get what he or she wants. Then, finally, begrudgingly, acceptance of rules and consequences takes place.

PUNISHMENT IS A LEARNED BEHAVIOR

Think about this logic: a child hits his little brother, so the parent hits the child to teach him not to hit his brother. This cyclical thinking does not make sense on a number of levels. However, what a child learns is, "I cannot hit the big adult and win. I cannot hit my brother and win. Then whom can I hit and win?" This may become a reason for gaining the upper hand by picking on a peer at school.

Also, in the tired world of parenting, this type of punishment approach is highly variable and subjective. "If I am angry, you will get a really good beating. If I am happy, I'll let you get away with it this time." Alternatively, "I am exhausted, so I cannot bother punishing you." Or, "I am full of energy, so today I am going to teach you a real lesson!" As a result, punishment becomes an inconsistent and uncertain matter of going between two very different extremes despite similar or identical actions by the child.

In addition, in a study by Catherine A. Taylor et al. (2018) and Janet C. Rice in the *Journal of Pediatrics*, it was found that spanking or corporal punishment leads to increased aggression in children.[1] Where does this aggression generally come out? In the place where they can find those less powerful than themselves—namely, in the school environment.

THE SCOURGE OF SUBSTANCE ABUSE

Substance abuse has always been a persistent issue that creates havoc on the family dynamic. The United States is experiencing an epidemic of drug overdose (poisoning) deaths. Since 2000, the rate of deaths from drug overdoses has increased by 137 percent, including a 200 percent increase in the rate of overdose deaths involving opioids (opioid pain relievers and heroin).[2] Further, according to the website DrugAbuse.com, "Drug use in America has swelled from 2002 to 2012. In 2002, 13.0% of Americans aged 12 or older had used an illicit drug or medication in the past month. By 2012, that number had increased to 13.2%—an increase of over 4 million people."[3]

With these increases in substance abuse, so correlates a mushrooming of domestic violence, other crimes, as well as child abuse and neglect. As educators, our ability to influence the home life may be limited. That being said, however, if you have a "suspicion" of abuse, it is imperative to contact your local child protective services agency.

Often, educators are hesitant to make these calls. The worry is that we will disrupt the family to an even greater extent and/or we will be responsible for that child being removed from the household (to perhaps an even worse situation). Of course, there is also the concern that we are now going to be involved in the situation and in the crosshairs of anger and resentment from the family.

On the flip side, however, educators are the most likely persons to recognize abuse and neglect outside the home setting. Those in various professional-related fields submitted more than one-half (56.5 percent) of the abuse/neglect cases referred to protective services, with educators being most common source of generating these reports (16.2 percent).[4] If you are in doubt, it is always better to err on the side of caution and suspicion. Not only is it our legal and ethical obligation, but you can also put your "head on the pillow at night" knowing you have done your duty in protecting the child entrusted in your care.

THE HOMES HIERARCHY OF NEEDS

In every school, every town, and every district, children regularly live without electricity, water, or enough food. Now, as an educator in a wealthier district you may say, "Well, those are in those less financially advantaged districts. Not ours, right?"

Wrong! Have you ever been surprised by the seemingly perfect couple deciding to call it quits? Then, you hear of a hair-raising story of deceit, betrayal, and other astounding issues between the two. You think, they looked like they had the perfect house, the perfect life. Now, the details of their story have enough intrigue for a virtual miniseries.

Well, so it goes with what happens inside the very homes of your students. The outside may look unblemished and pristine, while on the inside the family buckles under financial stressors and other critical aspects, such as need for utilities, love, and supervision that goes out the window. The parents, meanwhile, do everything they can to hold the false pretense of the *perfect life* as a false facade to those outside the bounds of their well-manicured McMansion.

So the question becomes, how is a student who does not have the following (see table 1.1) able to keep up behaviorally and academically with his or her age-appropriate peers?

Table 1.1. A Student's Hierarchy of Needs

Not Enough Food	How does a child do schoolwork when he or she is always hungry?
No Electricity	How can a child do work without seeing? How can the child heat the house so that he or she can sleep?
No Water	How does a child come to school when he or she can't shower and is worried that he or she will smell?
No Computer	In our technology-driven, Internet-connected world, how can a child keep up with his or her peers?
No Safety	If a child is always afraid of what could happen to them, their siblings, or their family, how do they focus on school? The focus is on their daily survival instead.

The question then becomes: How do we as a school or community get these student/family needs met? The more we are able to do this, the better a student is able to succeed and the less impact we will likely see behaviorally in school.

RULES AND RITUALS: THE TWO R'S OF HOME

How did you learn the rules of your home? Chances are as a child you learned by your parent teaching you cause (your behavior) and effect (consequence that results). As a product, over time that consistent message taught you how to function in a world that is governed by cause and effect.

Now imagine, you did not learn these rules. How would you function? You would continuously bang your head against the same proverbial obstacles until either your head was bloodied or you learned what the world was trying to teach you the hard way.

This can be the case for many of our students with behavioral issues. For example, let's go back to the picture of the overwhelmed parents. They are tired, at wit's end, and exhausted, due to the stressors that pour on them each day. It takes every last ounce of energy they have to slump back onto the couch after work.

Now, the child acts out. They are too tired to address it, so they let it go. The next day, however, after a full night's sleep, they are energized, and they come down on that child for the same behavioral issue. Conversely, let's suppose that the same parent is in a good mood. In that case, the child gets off easily. The next day, the parent has a bad day at work, so the child better watch out!

This teaches a child tacitly that consequences are unpredictably based on one's energy or emotion. Rather than look toward your behavior and potential logical consequence, you now must look at the unpredictable nature of one's parents' oscillating moods.

What if you want attention? In a household like this, the adage "Kids should be seen and not heard" is taken to an extreme. The aggravated parent wants to be left alone: "Play your tablet, play your video game, stay out of my hair." Conversely, the child wants to get attention from that distracted parent. So how does the child address these contrasting needs and wants?

Simple, the child misbehaves. In short, that negative attention gives "more bang for the buck" than the continued expected behaviors that positive behaviors bring. If a child misbehaves, he or she will be given the sole focus of the parent until the issue is remedied. The child essentially "forces the parent's hand" to pay attention to him or her, as creating a reaction to a negative is better than no attention at all.

Translate that to the school setting: a child comes to school and sees that he or she must vie for the attention of one teacher among twenty-four other peers. Clearly, good behaviors are not going to cut it. They will be lumped into the large number of nameless, faceless, "good kids." Behave negatively and you have the teacher, principal, school counselor, and half the adults of the school at your beck and call. Not to mention, your peers are also talking about you at every opportunity of the day.

Emotion in the home only serves to fuel this behavior. Why? Because when a parent models anger, to the youth's anger it simply ignites more anger. If you have ever seen a two-year-old tantruming in your local supermarket only to see a parent having a parallel tantrum right next to him or her, you have observed this formula.

RITUALS

Think about your happiest memories as a child. Maybe it is annual family trips, Thanksgiving dinners, or Christmas mornings. These are the rituals that create a foundation of predictability, safety, and bonding among all family members.

Rituals, however, require the need for vision and routine. If a family is chaotic and unpredictable, by their very nature they cannot have a routine that fosters rituals. Therefore, children with chaotic families are in a perpetual state of anxiety. For some, that uneasiness shows up in the most often-utilized emotion of anger.

In school, we naturally embrace rituals. Each and every school year, we have holiday parties and decorate for special events. Keep in mind that these rituals are vital for at-risk students who simply do not have this level of stability versus some of your other pupils.

POST TRAUMA OF HOME TO SCHOOL

There is often the notion that children are "resilient." That is, they have the flexibility in childhood to go through a great deal of traumatic events and come out on the other end seemingly unscathed. They are infinitely flexible and malleable; they bend but don't break.

It is true that children do have an ability to handle things during their development, within reason. However, there is a basis as to why we often hear of posttraumatic stress; because it occurs *after* the fact. This means a child does not have a choice but to handle a distressing event when it occurs; it is a necessary skill for survival.

All of us have this, when we have an emergent event happen. We muster all of our strength and energy for the issue at large. Then, a day, a week, or a month later, we fall apart when it is safer to have the opportunity. So it is with children. In a school setting, you may see the results of posttrauma within your class where it may indeed be the only safe environment for the child to "fall apart."

Testing, you as the educator, may take place as to how you are going to handle emotions that may simply not be safe to express at home. The means by which we assist students in expressing/addressing these emotions are vital in how the pupil ultimately handles anger and posttraumatic development.

YOUR NORM MAY NOT BE THE FAMILIES' NORM

How do you define "normalcy"? That is, what is normal, acceptable, or appropriate?

Likely, this came from your parents, extended relatives, and/or some level of solid role models within your life. In addition, it may have stemmed from a value system of religious or spiritual values. Yet, what if you had none of these? How skewed may your perception of so-called normalcy be?

In some families, generational issues of domestic violence, drug use, or even varying other forms of abuse have run rampant. All of these are, obviously, horrible and detrimental to the erosion of the family and the individual alike.

Nevertheless, with poor role modeling, some fall into the crevices of the very same behaviors of a past generation. Why? Because it has been accepted, normalized, minimized, or, at worst, rationalized.

When this occurs, it can be accepted as something that "just is." Why does this affect you as an educator? Because you cannot simply assume that a family knows what can be deemed conventional: societal norms or your own norms. People can't assimilate what they have never been taught. This goes for all forms of learning and education: the public school as well as the school of hard knocks.

CULTURE IN THE HOME: THE BACKGROUND MUSIC OF YOUR PUPILS IN THE SCHOOL

We are all from a culture—more specifically, an idiosyncratic blend of cultures. The cultures influence our lives and bleed together like watercolors on a rich tapestry that is the canvas of one's life.

Cultures are what enrich our existence, teach us rituals, and, to a degree, create the norms of life. That being said, cultures vary to degrees of almost infinite proportions. Cultures form in schools that lead to each building having a specific cultural fingerprint in each and every school in our nation. Often we talk about "school culture," but do we talk about the "cultures of the school"? That is, perhaps, more vital than the often-used term "school climate."

Understanding and embracing the various cultures that encompass your school and its student body may be helpful by recognition of the following:

- *Some cultures equate educators with such reverence that they don't question authority:* In some cultures, the educator is not to be questioned. This means that in dialogue in which you are asking for differing perspectives or contrasting views, they will not answer for fear of clashing with your knowledge or disrespecting your authority (i.e., country).
- *Each school district has its own idiosyncratic population of cultures:* Look at your local department of education's statistics, and you can find population data. This can be one measure of understanding the cultural dynamic.
- *Attempt to understand and embrace your understanding of cultures: in cultural contexts, you don't know what you don't know:* For instance, you can make a cultural indiscretion by simply shaking the hand of an opposite-sex pupil whose culture forbade it. Wrongly interpreted, it can be deemed that the pupil is standoffish and rude. Understand before you interpret one's behavior.
- *Encourage, whenever possible, diverse curriculum:* Students or faculty not understanding pupils' individualistic cultures can create issues of potential unneeded discord or, worse harassment and bullying.

OPINION OF EDUCATION

If you have become an educator, clearly you put the importance of learning on a pedestal. Don't make the mistake, however, and think that everyone else holds education in the same high regard as you do. Some families just don't find education to be of the same vital nature as you might.

Further, if a child had a bad educational experience, then he or she likewise will have that same framework toward his or her child attending school. In addition, most families can base their opinion only on what they know. This view (as we addressed earlier) is what they bring to the feeling about school.

WHEN CUTE IS NO LONGER CUTE

When a child says his or her first words, parents are transfixed with this most adorable milestone. As they verbally stumble and say words in an awkward or incorrect fashion, some parents are hesitant to correct them for fear that they "are growing up." Now, picture for a moment that a child picks up the profanity that he or she hears in a household from others. Generally, three responses are possible: (1) ignore the child, (2) laugh at how "cute" it is that the child is using adult language, or (3) reprimand the child and try to reduce his or her using profane language.

Most parents will try to immediately cease this language via correcting the child and then trying to be more cognizant of what they say in front of little ears. However, there are a handful of parents who use profanity as much as we use any other noun or adjective, and so they (and the child) become immune to this language. Others support this language by laughing it off as cute (until the child attempts it at school). Yet, others pay so much undue attention to the words that they inadvertently reinforce what it is they want to try to stop because the child associates the "word or words" with negative attention.

WHEN CHILDREN DON'T LEARN THE LANGUAGE OF BEING A CHILD AT HOME

Imagine that you are plopped on a planet where no one speaks your language. Your sense of humor is foreign to them, the way you interact is strange to them, and your ability to understand their customs is also odd to their way of thinking.

So is the case with an only child or one who has a decade-or-so age gap from his or her eldest sibling. Imagine for a moment the vantage point from a child who is an only child or significantly youngest child.

How does a child learn conflict resolution? He or she learns it from siblings. The child adapts to give and take, sharing and cooperating, boundaries, and recognizing another's property. Adults, on the other hand, are far more forgiving to kids. We give them what they want, we let them win, and sometimes we even give them things that are not rightfully theirs.

How does a child learn socialization? Children have their own ways of thinking and interacting that are often subtle to the adult human eye. When they play in a group, they do not let others play until they are generally completed with the activity. They tend to have concrete senses of humor (which is why their jokes are often not very funny). Now, you have a child whose only exposure to the world is by which adults talk and from that adult lens. The child then applies adult humor in a child's world with very poor results. The attention and boundaries that the child desires are now shared among other peers.

AMERICAN IDLE THREATS

Often in these households, consequences are couched in empty threats. These threats then lead the youth to believe that the family is not serious.

Alternatively, at times, the threats are overly harsh and create a "seesaw" effect, in which the child has a parent come down very hard on him or her, and, simultaneously, the other parent lets him or her get away with proverbial murder due to guilt and believing he or she needs to "balance" the perceived harshness of the other parent (or vice versa).

1. The issue then becomes that the child really, again, has no idea of what rules, boundaries, or consequences are.
2. The cause-and-effect nature of a behavior for a child is never completely understood because parents block the child from either understanding the cause or experiencing the effect. Or, they are given the mixed "seesaw" message.

This is generally not the way a classroom (nor society) functions. In society, citizens adhere to a definitive list of rules and respective group of consequences accordingly. It is difficult to understand a stable list of rules and consequences if they are always variable, changing, and unpredictable (as they are in these households).

RESPONSIBLE FOR NOTHING

When a family feels beaten down by society, they can either figure out a means to change what they are doing or they can blame the world around them. Chronically, in many aspects of politics, sports, and entertainment, we see an epidemic of failure to take responsibility for one's actions.

This has filtered down to the family dynamic as well. In many instances it is simply too painful or requires too much effort to take responsibility for one's actions. It is far easier to blame an outside entity, whether it be extended family, society, or educators. The issue becomes that when children are encouraged to not be responsible for their actions, they are unable to recognize how to solve problems or determine a means of gaining self-esteem based on standing on their own two feet to address issues.

Hence, the concept of responsibility is a character trait that must be taught to both student and parent alike.

NOTES

1. Taylor, Catherine A., Fleckman, J. M., Scholer, J. J., Branco, N. "U.S. Pediatrics, Attitudes, Beliefs, and Perceived Norms About Spanking." Journal of Behavioral Pediatrics, 2018.

2. Leonard J. Paulozzi, Christopher M. Jones,, Karin A. Mack, and Rose A. Rudd, "Vital Signs: Overdoses of Prescription Opioid Pain Relievers—United States, 1999–2008," *Morbidity and Mortality Weekly Report* 60 (2011): 1487–92.

3. "Drug Abuse Statistics," DrugAbuse.com, August 13, 2016, drugabuse.com/library/drug-abuse-statistics/.

4. Child maltreatment 2015. Published January 2018. An Office of the Administration for Children of Families, a division of U.S. Department of Health & Human Services. This report represents national data about child abuse and neglect known to child protective services agencies in the United States during fiscal year 2016. Retrieved from: https://www.acf.hhs.gov/cb/resource/childmaltreatment-2018.

Chapter 2

The Parents

It All Starts Here

Parents are the ultimate role models for children. Every word, movement and action has an effect. No other person or outside force has a greater influence on a child than the parent.

—Bob Keeshan

"There goes the phone again," thinks Mr. Smith as he is jolted up by the shrill of the phone as it rings. He rubs his bleary eyes, grabs his glasses, and stares at his cell phone. Across the screen flashes Williamstown Elementary School. It is the eighth time this month that they called.

Mr. Smith has a flash of anger as he stares at the all too familiar number. "That school!" Mr. Smith thinks. "What he needs to do, what he does not do . . . but do they know what I am doing? I am working three jobs since their mother left. I have been taking them to school, counseling, feeding them, caring for them, and doing the best I can to raise them! At the same time, I have given up sleep, food, and everything to be the best dad I can!"

He thinks about letting the phone go to voice mail so he can get an hour or two of sleep before he heads off to work. Yet, he answers the phone (yet again) in a huff. "Hello!" On the other line is the principal, whom he can detect, exhibiting a judgmental and negative tone. "It is Ms. Jones again. Timmy has refused to follow his teacher's directions, thrown over a student's desk, and hit a peer . . . we need you to come pick him up. He is out of control, and we simply cannot have that here in our school!"

Mr. Smith begins to say that he is doing everything he can with his son to help him. He wants to say that he is just lucky that he can keep a roof over the family's head and food on the plate. He wants to tell the principal, "Do you know what our family has been through?" In his mind he imagines telling

19

"those people" at the school, "When he is here, he is my problem . . . when he is there, he is all yours!"

Mr. Smith bites his tongue; he throws on some clothes and picks up his son. Another day of missed work, missed money, and potentially being fired due to his "spotty" attendance record.

IT ALL STARTS HERE

The role of the parent in shaping every aspect of a child (positive as well as negative) cannot be understated. These are the people they spend the majority of their lives with. Despite you seeing them six hours per day, the parents are the ones who occupy the majority of their time, control, sculpt, and influence in the first several and critical years of development.

PARENTS DO THE BEST THEY CAN WITH WHAT THEY HAVE

The job of parenting is a very difficult one. Most parents do the very best with what they have. However, the odds are very much stacked against them. Social media, bullying, substance abuse, and financial issues all compound in a frenetic rate to make the job of parenting in the twenty-first century an uphill battle.

Don't get me wrong; there are parents who don't fulfill their roles, who abuse, who neglect, and who simply abandon the sacred role of being a caretaker to the children they are blessed and entrusted with. This being said, however, don't become jaded to think that these parents represent any sort of majority of the parents you work with. It becomes very easy to begin to believe this notion and fall into a "parent-blaming" perspective for all difficult students. That, in fact, is counterproductive to ultimately reaching both children and their families. It also will eventually burn you out when you believe it is merely a parental issue and you cannot do anything to make change in a child's life in the dynamics of a school environment when the home life is so dysfunctional.

Three Types of Parenting Styles

- *The permissive parent:* These parents tend to have very loose, overly flexible rules or have no rules at all. These parents will enforce a rule for one minute and not for the next.

    Imagine you are fearful to fly and get on a plane with a novice pilot. You fully recognize the pilot's uncertainty and immediately feel the hair on the back of your neck stand up, and you feel a pit in your stomach. You have essentially placed your life in the hands of someone who is, perhaps, not competent.

So is the permissive parents' view from the perspective of a child. Since they can't (or won't) place boundaries on the child, the child will test who can or who will. The child maybe testing the parent, the educator, or whoever will give him or her the boundaries that he or she needs to know so that he or she remains safe on the uncertain road of childhood.

Rules are as follows:

o   Rules are applied sporadically or inconsistently.
o   Children are free to make own rules.
o   Most infractions of rules are treated as "no big deal."
o   "Nothing is the child's fault."

* *The restrictive parent:* These parents are on the other side of the spectrum. They are overly rigid and strict. As youth age, they should be provided gradually more responsibilities. Rules and roles must adapt accordingly. Without these rules adapting, children outgrow these inflexible guidelines like a child outgrowing clothes too tight, "bust out" in frustration and anger.

   These parents ignore a crucial rule of engineering; it is not a structure that remains rigid in the strongest gale winds. Rather, it is best to create a structure that has some level of flexibility and give elasticity, to avoid snapping, due to its lack of flexibility.

Rules are as follows:

o   Rigid and unbending rules, despite child's level of trust and age.
o   Rules are enforced with fear, reactivity, and forceful emotion(s).
o   "Everything is child's fault" (even issues that are the between parents or due to anger or the emotionality of one or both of the parents).

* *The democratic parent:* This parent is somewhat of a hybrid between the two discussed previously. They have rules that are clear, concise, and consistent. Yet, those rules are able to be tailored and adapted toward the children based on age, personality, and ability to take responsibility for one's actions.

   The democratic parenting style allows for a child to grow and learn while simultaneously understanding the confines, roles, and responsibilities of being a member of the family. They have opportunities to address conflict in a productive manner, express emotions, and feel as a valued member of the family dynamic.

Rules:

o   are clear, concise, consistent, and logical.
o   adapt to growing needs and responsibilities as the child(ren) age(s).
o   applied in a manner that is not overly reactive.

THE PARENTING BALANCE

Often when a child has a rigid view on parenting and/or a child has been through traumatic issues such as being witness to parental domestic violence, you see a "seesaw" effect—that is, a parent will be overly lenient to compensate for the issues of the other parent and vice versa.

This creates a cyclic effect, where one parent becomes harsher and, in turn, the other parent becomes more lax due to guilt and to "compensate." This creates more confusion as the child is "tossed around" by the confusion of the disparity in parenting rules.

AVOID THE LEAKY PIPE

If you were told that you had a pipe with a large crack in it, would you continue to let the water flow and watch the water gush out? Hopefully, you recognize that your water bill will continue to climb as the damage to your house rises exponentially and then find a shutoff valve to stop the water from bleeding you and your wallet dry.

TOP TWELVE DIFFICULT PARENTAL TYPES

1. *"My Child Is an Angel and You Are All at Fault" Parent*

    Basically, this type of parent believes that their child is "perfect." To admit otherwise will indicate, in their opinion, that they are deeply flawed as a parent. They project that any issue that takes place with faculty, students, or administration is turned around to be the fault of someone else besides their child.

    • These parents choose to stand in the way of their child experiencing the consequences of their actions. What parents such as these fail to realize is that they prevent their child's comprehension of cause and effect and logic and consequence. They see educators and their fellow peers in very stark tones. This means that the parents look at the world as either an "enemy" or a "friend." They will see teachers, administrators, and other children as "friends" or "enemies" of their child. In turn, an enemy of their child is an enemy of themselves.

- These parents are easily reactive. Therefore, they will be very emotional when they come into school. Mirroring any type of the emotional reactivity is a recipe for a whirlpool of disaster. When they get louder, your voice softens. When they yell, you patiently listen (unless they become overly belligerent and threatening).

- These parents become emotional very quickly. When they become emotional, logic goes out of the window. Create a mantra, a very deliberate and specific short message that you want them to gain from this interaction. Remember, the more steam coming out of their ears, the less of a message they will get from your dialogue. Make it short, make it useful, make it calm and repetitive while making it the one message you want that parent to take away from the meeting.

- Do not allow a parent's emotional nature to intimidate or frighten you into giving up your values or violating policies. These parents can attempt to overpower you and back you into a proverbial corner. In doing so, you may inadvertently give up values and/or "cut corners" on policy adherence. Don't; they will also hold you accountable for the "favor" you did. Hold steadfast to your values.

- Don't meet these parents alone. These families see those against them as an "enemy." In turn, they can be unpredictable and dangerous. The last thing you want is a "he said/she said" with them. Even if you win, you still have doubt in the far harsher court of public opinion.

- Document with these families. Remember, facts do matter with these families. Because when they are reactive, you have facts, dates, and times at your disposal.

- Do not e-mail these parents, if possible. Ever misconstrue a text, e-mail, or social media post? These families always see the negative in communication. Since a large percentage of interactions are nonverbal, the tone of the message becomes a big issue. Use e-mail only if you are trying to document something, not as a means of discussion. Save it for "one-way" dialogue only, when you are trying to document a message.

- Children who are provided this type of "you are an angel" parenting will often "triangulate" parents against teachers, administrators, or other persons. Triangulation involves having two parties (i.e., parent and educator) against each other and watching the "emotional fire-works" fly.

- They have learned that if they play the teacher against their parent, they can slink away while the attention of all is shifted to the conflict at hand. The payoff? The child and the consequences that could be applied are forgotten about, in lieu of all the emotional discord surrounding the situation.
- Avoid giving these students an opportunity to lie. These children have learned that manipulating the truth often helps to insulate themselves from consequences. As an example, we ask the child a question out of knee-jerk habit: "Did you do that?" Now, the "angelic" child has a choice: first, the child could say, "I did it," and risk a consequence, or second, he or she could lie and say, "I didn't do it" (after all you asked). This may help skirt him or her out of potential punishment on the off chance you believe him or her.

2. *The "When in School, He or She Is Your Problem" Parent*

Ever have the parents you call repeatedly, due to their child's behavior, and the responses you get like crickets, no call back, no answer, or, sometimes, you are met with a disconnected number altogether? If you do happen to reach these parents, they may offer empty compliance or, more likely, will never call you back.

- If a parent does not comply with helping you, do not immediately become defensive. When a family is drowning in an ocean of problems, fear, and debt and/or just hoping to survive moment to moment, they will not be able to see the life preserver of assistance that you put right in front of them. If those basic needs (food, money, clothing, utilities, etc.) are not being met, offer to have the social worker or school counselor help them to get these basic needs addressed. If these needs are addressed, then the parents will be better able to assist you with what you need from them in order to work collaboratively for the benefit of their child.
- These parents simply may believe that it isn't within their role to help with the child in regard to your concerns when they're in the educational environment. These parents take the tact, "I take care of them when they are with me and don't ask you for help, so when they are there, they are not my responsibility."
- If this is the case, and you have tried several times to contact the family to no avail, stop trying. You are wasting your time, irritating

yourself and your colleagues, and whittling away critical time/
resources to create useful strategies within the school.

- Consider creation of rewards that can be used in school and exclusive
  of the home. Sometimes we may have to "dig deep" to find creative
  means of developing these motivators.
- Develop a mentoring program whereas an adult whom they look up
  to can guide them and provide one-on-one attention.
- Find out what the parent does need. Many of this type of parents
  believe that the public school system represents a resource for the child
  and neglects to realize that the school can also help a parent in need.
- Try to monitor these families monthly for changes. These parents
  are often in a constant state of flux. Their residence, phone number,
  and/or relational statuses change. Not having this information current can pose an emergent situation, should there be a need to contact them quickly.

3. *The "Know It All" Parent*

These parents are perpetual questioners. They question every aspect of
the educational program, the faculty decisions, and why each and every
step is taken in relation to their child's educational career.
Many of these parents who fall into this category are engineers, math-
ematicians, or scientists and tend to view the world from the scope of a
critical and analytical eye. They navigate their world by inquiring about
the "black and white," the meaning (even when some things don't have
a clear "right" answer).

- These parents have a strong need to know what is going on in
  school. They abide by the motto, "An educated customer is a good
  customer." They need to understand how and what their child is
  learning and why. They must understand how things fit into the
  larger system of their child's knowledge of the world.
- Many special education parents are especially knowledgeable (sometimes more so than the so-called professionals). Recognize that,
  though education is your profession, caring for a special education
  child is their "lifetime" role.
- Avoid taking these questions as attacks on your competence or abilities. Answer these questions in a polite and direct manner.
- If you are deviating from your traditional means of teaching or
  counseling in any manner, let these parents know, as they will be the
  first to question it. Get written permission before you deviate in any
  significant manner from curriculum or agendas.

- Proactively give information, and make it readily available via weekly newsletters or by consistently updating your website.
- Encourage questions and allow for open dialogue with these parents.

4. *The "Bully" Parent*

In some cases, the "apple doesn't fall far from the tree." In the case of "bullying parents," this may be so. In the past several years of public education, perhaps no subject has aroused greater interest, controversy, or change than that of harassment, intimidation, and bullying.

Many of us remember the childhood playground bully. The one who would shove you off the slide, tease you, tell others not to play with you, or threaten to give you "a knuckle sandwich" if you did not give him or her your ham sandwich at lunch. Well, these children are all grown up now, and some morph into "bullying" parents.

- Don't allow these parents to scare you into getting what they want. Just as the child bully intimidates the target into giving up what he or she wants, so does the adult parental bully. They learn that coming on hard and fast often intimidates and overpowers others into giving them what they want.

   Doing this, however, may calm the issue for a short period. The next issue will arise, sooner rather than later, and, again, you will have to either stand up or back down. The more you back down, however, the greater entitlement the bully parent feels to stand up. Eventually, either you violate your own values or policies in an all-out battle or you stand up early and set boundaries that demonstrate mutual respect for each other's roles.
- Call these parents first. If you wait for a child to go home and tell the parent his or her "side of the story," before you have a chance to speak, you are setting yourself up with the bully parents. Their children often are fearful of their parents' ire, and so they will say anything to get themselves out of hot water. Often, these parents react with anger versus logic first (remember logic is not emotional, and being emotional is not logical). Calling them proactively allows you to provide them a more balanced perspective of exactly what happened.
- If you have a short fuse, don't light yourself. Sometimes, we are all guilty of letting anger get the best of us. Bullying parents can bring back memories of bullying situations of yesteryear for ourselves

and can trigger reactive emotions. If you are going to get angry and say something you will regret, hold off. Remember, you cannot take back what you say, and these parents have long memories and will "roast" you in the court of public (and public school) opinion without hesitation.

- Do not e-mail these parents except for the purpose of documentation. Remember, these parents already have a firm line drawn in the sand. They seek "targets" for their frustration and venom. So they comb through e-mails to look for any subtle message of attack. Guess what? When they look hard enough, they find some ambiguous part of your e-mail that they can take in a negative fashion and react accordingly. That is not to say absolutely never e-mail parents. If you need a means of documentation, e-mail can be the most effective way of doing so.
- These parental meetings always have the smoldering potential to quickly becoming explosive. If emotions do boil over and spill into rage, the meeting may cease being effective. Stop the meeting, and consider rescheduling it. If steam is coming out of the ears, there is nothing productive going into the parents' brain, so let them blow off some steam in the meantime.
- Remember, these "bully" parents attempt to get small issues pushed across, and then they pick up steam when they recognize this strategy works for them. Now, with a false sense of entitlement, these parents may attempt to further push their agenda with larger and more critical issues.
- Don't find yourself playing "catch-up" and trying to reestablish or set boundaries too late with these parents. They generally will be the first to point out, "But you (or someone else in charge) made an exception the last time." These parents will only respect strength from the onset, not negotiation that is falsely perceived as a weakness to them. Also, avoid getting into the trap of comparing their child to the way that a former student was handled. Each pupil is handled in a consistent but tailored means, and you must assure them that you will not violate or discuss another child's confidentiality because they have brought that discussion into the picture.

5. The "My Child Will Attend School When He or She Wants To" Parent

One can garner a great deal of information by just looking at the pattern of attendance. If they are out Mondays, it could be the family has difficulty transitioning from late night/late wakening of weekends. Several days off in a row can be (by *no means* definitive) keeping a possibly abused child home for bruises to heal, a parental drug binge, or as an innocuous, as a vacation.

- At times, educators in well-intentioned frustration will elect to not provide work to do at home to those pupils who are chronically absent. This is counterproductive, as it does not allow a student who may want to keep up with work the ability to do so. Urge school work to be provided as long as the parent picks it up. Remember, it is our vision to teach all of our students (not to withhold education) regardless of potential circumstances.
- If you suspect a child is being abused or neglected, it is your legal and ethical duty to report. Remember, it is neither your place nor duty to determine or investigate fully what is going on. Leave this role to the child welfare experts who specialize in this area. It is your job to refer based on a "suspicion" of possible abuse/neglect.
- At times, faculty comes across youth who do have true school phobia. If so, when they do come to school, let them feel welcome. Do not shame the students or have yourself or their peers pepper them with inquiries as to where they were or allow their peers to run wild with speculation, rumor, or gossip about them. Doing so with others around only serves to exacerbate school-related anxiety issues.
- Seek assistance from the school social worker or counselor. At times, such as these, it will take more than pushing the issue from a solely classroom-based perspective. This student may need school counseling in collaboration with outpatient counseling and parental enrichment skills to fully support the student in a way that assures maximum success. This may even include a temporarily shortened school day, or schedule modification, to help the child build/develop the courage to come to school and to decrease the anticipatory anxiety, given ultimate success. With the vital element that parents understand if a child ceases coming to school at all, the mountains of school anxiety will only rise higher and become increasingly more difficult for their son/daughter to climb.
- Is the parent home? If the parent is home, this is one of the telltale signs that a student will be wanting to stay home. Students often will feel they are missing something that a parent is doing when they are home. If a parent has a chronic illness, they may find the need to help the parent. Assuring a student (as well as the parent) of the legal and educational role of a student being in school is vital for understanding for child and parent alike.
- Involve the attendance officer early. The attendance officer can be an amazing internal resource/advocate who can bridge the chasm

between home and school. Regular contact with the attendance officer will determine what the parent or child may not be telling you such as the condition of the house, financial utility needs, issues of neglect, as well as emotional and health issues that may be present for the parents.

- Consider going out with the attendance officer. It is unwise for a number of reasons to go to a family's residence alone. However, going with a secondary person such as the attendance officer can help you learn an infinite amount about a child and his or her family that you simply cannot learn in the relative sterile environment that can be the public school domain, which also serves as a second set of documentation of events.

6. The "Not My Child" Parent

These parents continue to grow exponentially and have turned the idea that "the teacher is always right" on its head. This old-school mentality existed less than a generation ago. However, these parents are leaving the adults and authority figures to prove themselves under the fickle eye of the youth.

"Not my child" parents have difficulty indicating that their child is responsible for anything because they see their child in the limited lens of their home, without any other peer interactions or any responsibilities (i.e., schoolwork) placed upon them. They have placed their child on such a high pedestal that they cannot see the whole child in the clouds of their own misguided and unbalanced glimpse of their child.

- When their child is criticized, they take it directly as an attack against themselves. They see this as a hurtful blow to their own psyche and as a criticism of their own parenting (in addition to an insult to their family). In such a case, we must allow them to recognize "normalized" child/student behavior. To be more specific, we need to let parents know that children are expected (by all of us) to make mistakes as a manner of learning and growing. It does not mean that the parent is at fault for a child making a faulty decision on the road to eventual adulthood.
- Educate the parent on board policies and procedures. This takes the conversation away from blaming toward the more "black and white" yardstick of rules and regulations. These parents often believe you are "victimizing" their child and their family. This strives away from a perceived personal attack against them, their child, and their family.

- Don't speak first. Allow the parent the opportunity to speak first before you talk. First, it "takes some wind out of their sails" of anger, so to speak, while you look for a point of agreement. Wait long enough and it is there! If you agree with any point of their argument, use it as a starting point. Remember, this does not mean you necessarily agree wholeheartedly with them just that you can see their viewpoint in a particular area. With the "Not My Child" parent they are looking for you to agree and to be an ally to them, while they are hanging on to every word that indicates you are with or against them for the conflict at hand. Finding a common theme helps prepare that foundation upon which to work together.
- It is highly suggested that you have another faculty member (e.g., the assistant principal or school social worker) present in meetings, to have further documentation, should the parent become angered or begin to "point fingers" and use verbal daggers. These parents can become angry quickly, so plan initially and accordingly with backup in mind.

7. *The "Passive-Aggressive" Parent*

When you first meet these parents, they seem to be overly kind, and you tend to may even want to let your "professional guard down." They pour the compliments on thick and heavy. These parents are perpetually available to help seemingly at every turn or activity. They give the best gifts at holidays to the teachers and secretaries.

They are generally heavily involved in the school, organizations, and social media. These parents may troll the school for gossip or to establish relationships with teachers so that they can try to push from educator to bordering on as a friend. They are always seeking to "blur" those boundaries and lay in waiting for the hapless educator who will fall into this trap.

- Be aware of gifts (even small ones). The price of a coffee or a bagel may seem minute. However, with these parents, it is a large sum that the educator may pay. It is a key to begin to open the boundary between professionalism and friendship. Please know, many parents give out of the goodness of their heart without any expectation of anything in return. These parents, however, see this as a transactional activity; "I give you something . . . I get something in return." Therefore, this seemingly inexpensive token of appreciation then becomes more of an expensive gift of trying to establish a bond like the apple put on a teacher's desk hoping to be the teacher's pet.

- Be careful of backhanded compliments. A passive-aggressive parent generally uses compliments as a means of comparison or opportunity versus to deliver an actual message of kindness. For instance, "You are a much better principal/teacher than Ms. so and so." The hope? By not defending the other or accepting this compliment, inadvertently, you may set up this parent to state that you side with his or her view of the other.
- Remember the pendulum swings both ways with these parents. These parents tend to view the world in "black and white." Rarely, do they see the "gray area"; that is, an educator (or any person) can be average; he or she doesn't have to be the "best or worst, enemy or ally." Hence, if you are "the best teacher ever" and they sing your praises, they are just as likely to quickly swing in the other direction and classify you are "the worst ever." If you need support of this theory, look at the history that such parents have left behind with former educators. If you see a trail of teachers who have been bad-mouthed and were terrible to a family or the student, it may be that it is just a matter of time before you are tossed into that bin of "bad" educators who did not see their point of view and "betrayed" them.
- Avoid these parents at all cost, be it social media or the soccer field. Remember, these parents are entrenched in many community organizations and social media. By getting wrapped up with these parents and not maintaining strong boundaries, you may be in for a whole world of hurt in the judgmental and gossip-filled world of social media or in the field of soccer moms and dads. These parents also like to "volunteer" and can often seek places where teachers congregate (i.e., the faculty room, work room). They are not generally "invited" in these places; however, they know this is where they can get the latest school gossip.

8. *The "Why Does Everyone Always Pick on My Child" Parent*

These parents question as to why their child is always victimized by the students, faculty, or both. Oftentimes, however, these parents frequently become "Bullying" parents or "My Child Does No Wrong" parents depending on how the issue and relationship evolve or dissolve.

- Do not allow these parents to take the conversation of behavioral issues with their child toward blaming or victimization. These parents tend to address things in very emotional terms. They see their child as a "victim" and the one whom they deem to be antagoniz-ing their child as "the enemy." Remind them that it is the behavior that you are addressing, not condemning another child's character, or, consequently, the alleged bully parents' parenting skills. If you do so, it goes down an emotional road and provides little in the way of solutions.

- Avoid being overreactive or babbling on and on. Too much babbling or being emotional only serves to mud the waters with these families and creates the feeling that they are being victimized and attacked. Listen carefully while not invoking too much in the way of emotions or words with these parents.
- Encourage rules and consequences that are consistent across classrooms. It is difficult to understand and/or enforce rules and consequences when each teacher has a chasm of contrasting rules, expectations, and consequences for seemingly identical issues. Be certain that your teachers have somewhat consistent rules and con-sequences throughout the building.

Why? Because how can you possibly apply rules and consequences in a school when each classroom has their own manner of rules, con-sequences, and expectations? Further, this allows these parents to highlight the school's lack of consistency in its handling of issues.

9. *The "Helicopter Parent"*

These parents are named for their predisposition to "hover" around their children like helicopters seeking a helipad. These parents may be considered overly involved and don't allow their children to fully grow and experience the learning that only cause and effect and life experi-ence can bring. As a result, they may have children who are emotion-ally immature or try to be sneaky in order to avoid having to sneak under the parental helicopter blades of rigid and inflexible rules.

- These parents do not trust that their children are safe or capable. These parents have difficulty "letting go." They have anxiety (that is often transferred to the child as well) that their children may not be equipped to handle life without constant and consistent parental contact. Contact the parents (or have the teacher or school coun-selor do so) on a regular basis initially to assure their child is being successful. If you say to yourself, "I don't have time for that," trust me if you do not call at your earliest convenience, you will get calls from the parents of an "urgent" nature frequently at their convenience.

- Compliment the parents for their genuine concern for their child. All parents have a genuine concern for their child. These parents are fearful, however, that their child is ill equipped for the "real world." Ironically, their parenting strategy creates a self-fulfilling prophecy. Assure them that you recognize their good intentions.
- Report successes to the parents. These parents are concerned that their child cannot succeed without their constant assistance and interventions. Hence, when their child does succeed, that is a perfect opportunity to use these achievements to help allay their fears.
- Call these parents back as soon as you can. These parents "hover" because they are anxious and ruminate on how a trivial issue may be a calamity for their child. If you call them and leave a message, assure them that the call is not an emergency. If they call you, try to call them back as soon as possible. If you do not, they are likely to venture up the chain of command trying to get an answer to what they believe is a critical issue that must be handled instantly.

10. *The "Distrustful of Public Education/Special Education" Parent*

Think back to when you were in school; how much has changed? What if you never entered the field of education? You would believe that public school was similar (or the same) as your previous frame of reference. Whether it be academic issues, a lack of focus on public education, or having been in the special education system themselves, some parents are not inherently trusting of public education and come with an attitude that is one of defensiveness and inherent lack of trust.

- Avoid meetings in which several faculty members are saying similar things to the parents that are negative or critical of their child. How many meetings have you been in when several faculty members say the same critique of how a student is performing poorly in school? One person can say this, and it does not have to be echoed by everyone else. Therefore, be somewhat proactive as to who will say what.
- Don't focus on being right or wrong; focus on what is right for the student. Oftentimes, both parties get caught in the nonproductive cycle of "being right." We must ask ourselves when we enter that power struggle, what are we doing productively that is "right" for the student?
- Look for opportunities of mutual agreement. If we can, have the parent "save face" and find a chance to meet halfway toward an optimal solution, which is commonly called a "win-win" solution.

- Some of these parents may have been in special education programs themselves. Remember when you were in school? There tended to be a stigma and segregation associated with special education pupils. Consequently, if you received special education services during that time, you may feel that this is the same paradigm used in current special education programs. Therefore, if you are going to discuss that special education is not the same as few years ago, that is simply not enough; you must show them. They need to see what kind of class their child will be in as they are skeptical of a system where they felt they were segregated from the so-called normal children. This means offering them an opportunity to see things differently with their own eyes.

11. *The "My Kid Is Bored" Parent*

This is a favorite of parents who are told that their child is not living up to the academic rigors of a particular class. This myth has been fostered due to a number of different issues.

- The time-tested and useless question is, "What did you do today in school?" What is the response? As you know if you have children (or have ever asked this question), the answer is usually some variant of "nothing . . . I don't know . . . not much." It is no wonder then that a parent would say their child is "bored." If nothing has broken the memory threshold of anything interesting, what would you think? Well, my child must be bored.
- It is important that we have constant communication with parents via newsletter, phone call, or websites that offer consistent and constant information regarding the school day. Doing so will allow parents to ask more pointed questions that will get more specific responses. Ultimately, this provides a better gauge of what their children are doing in school, and, consequently, they are less inclined to take verbatim that if their child says "We did nothing in school," it is, in fact, not the case.
- In the real world if you don't produce, you don't get reimbursed. Provide parents with an example in their own lives or occupations as it is useful. If you cannot produce in your job role, fact is your abilities are obsolete. Having ability and producing a product are two very different things.
- Consider that perhaps these students may perform better with technology as a means of demonstrating their academic abilities. Children of the twenty-first century tend to become "bored" because

their brains are wired into a world of technology, which is infinitely more visual and tactile in nature than most classroom settings. If possible, try to have the teacher use technology to see if the student will produce work that may not otherwise be garnered via paper-and-pencil task alone.

12. *The Substance-Abusing Parent*

With the upsurge of prescription medication abuse as well as traditional alcoholism and other illicit substances, it is always important to be aware of potentially impaired parents. Look for the following with these parents (this is by no means an all-inclusive list):

- Physical and emotional limitations
- Diminished ability of desire to meet a child's basic needs or wants
- Unstable mood, impulsivity, or behavior
- Inability to provide basic financial and support needs for themselves and/or their children
- Sudden change in work schedule or being fired from work
- Birth defects of children that may have been caused by previous substance abuse
- Separation from family and other social supports

Keep in mind that these parental types only represent a handful of the parents you may work with. Try to remember that many of these parents may be drowning in a sea of frustration or emotional, physical, and/or financial issues. Therefore, they will pull down anyone, or anything, that is around them (including you), in an attempt to keep their heads above the water.

When you interact with these parents, think about the priorities. We have only a limited amount of ammunition and power, and so you must decide if this is the issue/hill that you want to climb, regarding a parental issue. If you, therefore, are working with these parents, give them productive ideas as opposed to telling them what their student "can't do or their limits." Remind them that the goals of the school and the parents are ultimately the same: to do what is right for their child.

Chapter 3

The School

The Framework for the Future

There is much more to schools than buildings. There are academic activities, how it reaches the community and its proximity to other programs.

—John Warner

As she looks up from her hands wet with tears, she surveys the scene of her new school. She has never really grown "used" to any of her new schools, as this is the third one in three years.

Each time the routine is the same: she is the new student, the "new kid." Kids are superficially nice to her; however, at lunch, at recess, and on the bus everyone is sitting in their cliques that have been long formed over years of being together from preschool onward.

Everyone is nice to her initially until the "newness" wears off in a day or two. As they get to know her, they think she is a "control freak and bossy." They shy away from her. She believes they talk about her behind her back, and she hates the "drama" that each school harbors. In her thoughts, different schools, different students, same issues, same problems, same garbage.

But wait! This school seems slightly different. As she scans around, the school she notices is adorned with the accomplishments of the students. The teachers and students are wearing something that she has not seen in the schools of the past. It is not the latest fashion, the coolest cell phones; it is a look of happiness, contentment, and one of sincerity.

The students are quick to notice that she is a "wallflower" in what is a garden of familiar peers. They are eager to have her join their groups, and they embrace her. Of course, the teachers are also there to follow suit. For the first time, she feels comfortable, cared about, and well wanted.

Her world has been so upside down over the past three years since her mother left the boyfriend that beat both of them. She began to think that the world did not have a place for her. She felt as though she was an alien who had been dropped here from another planet and that she was awaiting to get to a place that was home, one where she was accepted.

Maybe, just maybe, this is the school for her? Maybe this is her place, her school, her family? A place in which she belonged to it and it to her?

A school is more than a brick-and-mortar building. Despite online education, it is the school climate, the faculty, and the students that make a school. It is the only place that the vast majority of our next generation will establish a framework of community under a single roof. It is where memories are formed, friendships are made, and self-esteem and lifelong learning are established.

Conversely, it can be a place of dread. The school can be something that children learn to fear—an environment in which teachers try to show that the "real world" is a place in which authority figures usurp all their power and are "out to get you for doing wrong," where punishment is doled out of mean spiritedness and not of teaching a lesson applicable to the real world, and where bullying creeps around like a cancerous mold in the outskirts of places unsupervised by educators, unseen, uncared for, as it festers and grows, to impact each and every pupil and faculty member present within its gangly grasp.

WHY IS IT IMPORTANT TO LOOK SO CLOSELY AT THE SCHOOL CONCERNING BEHAVIOR?

The school system is generally the first exposure a child has to the general society and the public at large. It is the first "system" that a child needs to learn to navigate and to function within accordingly. This, however, is just the start of a countless number of "systems" that they will have to be a part of as being a member of society. Therefore, the school is a microcosm of the larger society that they will one day inherit.

Hence, we must look at how children with behaviors adapt to their role in the educational community. This knowledge can be a good predictor of their ability to succeed in the larger community of life in the future that is laid out before them.

IT STARTS AT THE TOP

School climate starts at the very top. If an administrator is punitive, manipulative, or power hungry, the same characteristics are accepted and radiate their roots throughout a school. In turn, students who tend to have anxiety, anger, or other behavioral issues are more likely to harbor them in the educational setting as well.

It seems like common sense; however, students who have behavioral issues of any sort are keenly aware of any subtle changes or perceived "unfairness" within the school's systemic hierarchy. It is a survival skill to notice anything that may be changing or endanger their emotional or physical well-being. These students thrive on routine and understanding cause and effect as well as natural and logical consequences of actions. When they notice deviations in this, behaviors break out.

Not certain if this is true? Look at what happens before holidays, snowstorms, summer vacation, and/or any big event. Children can sense the excitement or changes; for some, they are able to contain it. For others, this becomes a catalyst for behavioral disruptions.

WHAT MAKE A GOOD "TOP-DOWN" ADMINISTRATOR FOR STUDENTS WITH BEHAVIORS?

- *Fairness:* By fairness, tailoring the fit as much as possible so that every student gets what they need. Avoiding making rash or sweeping decisions that are not in the best interests for the student at hand.
- *Patience and balance:* This is a simple one to note; however, it may be the one that is most difficult to change. In a 2010 report, *Churn: The High Cost of Principal Turnover*, it was determined that 25 percent of U.S. administrators quit their schools every year, and close to half leave in their third year.[1] Therefore, it is vital that an administrator has the ability to balance the job and have patience for the many facets that such a job entails.
- *Ability to discipline versus punish:* Can the administrator utilize the responsibility entrusted to him or her to enforce the rules and do so in a manner that is also educational in nature? For some, adults absolute power becomes a weapon for which to employ punishment versus teaching discipline to students for using mistakes as means of learning. Every opportunity in life is an opportunity to educate (especially in the area of mistake making).
- *Positive thinking:* It is easy for any educator to get drawn into negative thinking with the cynical political climate on public education, difficult parents, and the handful of faculty members who can be irritating and seek to spread negativity to those eager to be swayed. Yet, if the administrator subscribes to this negative thinking, it filters to everyone. Those students with behavioral or emotional issues who tend to be negative thinkers eventually are the ones left to filter that very negativity in their developing brains as they feed on the increasingly heavy layers of negativity that settle toward the bottom (namely, the students).

- *Ability to make others feel appreciated:* Feeling appreciated is a vital human need akin to air and water. If we do not feel needed or appreciated, our psyche slowly withers and dies. In fact, in a Globoforce survey that was referenced in a *Huffington Post* article in March 2017, 86 percent of employees who were recognized monthly say they "trust their boss." Whereas those workers who are not actively recognized note only 48 percent give their boss the benefit of trust.[2] If teachers don't trust their administrators, and we teach students who have behavioral as well as trust issues, what happens then?
- *Ability to convey a consistent message and vision:* In the daily grind of educational life, it can be a challenge in itself to just try to stay afloat. The challenge becomes for a relatively consistent vision to be portrayed to all educational stakeholders. When it is not this, it creates a school that is inconsistent from class to class, grade to grade, and creates a sense of chaos versus routine. An administrator must be able to "see the forest" for the proverbial trees and make systemic change and find uniform direction versus micromanage.

ARE RULES AND CONSEQUENCES CONSISTENT IN MOST ELEMENTS OF YOUR SCHOOL SETTING?

In the world of adults, we ideally strive for fairness and consistency. It is what we seek in terms of understanding the world around us. In fact, one may argue we have laws so that we can comprehend what are the expectations of society we must follow to succeed and not be penalized in a world that can be changing and unpredictable.

For example, when you are driving 85 mph in a 65 mph zone and get pulled over by the police officer, you can reasonably expect that you will receive a ticket and a certain amount of points whittled from your driver's license. Likewise, do it somewhere else in your state, and, though you may not know the speed traps, you can expect a roughly comparable consequence for your lead-footed behavior.

Let's translate that to the school setting. If I do something relatively innocuous, such as, say, chewing gum, what will my consequences be? Now, if you are a teacher who has a distinct pet peeve for the saliva-laden chomping of gum, you may provide a relatively harsh consequence. While the teacher next door? You can chomp away to your heart's delight. It is no bother, no worry.

This creates a distinct difficulty in terms of understanding the realm of expectations in school and, eventually, the so-called real world that adults always shake a foreboding finger toward students in ominously warning tones. Schools and teachers (including special areas) must conclude for similar parallel consequences that occur for comparable behaviors in different school classrooms as well as settings.

Schools must take a systemic view of school-district-wide effect, from teacher through to administrator. Otherwise, we have parents who question, "Why did my child do the same behavior as Student B and get a consequence that was twice as serious?" Now, we cannot discuss disciplinary measures in comparison to other peers; however, don't they have a point? Consequences and rules should be consistent among students and classes as much as possible to make rational sense and follow a consistent policy and procedure.

ARE RULES AND CONSEQUENCES APPROPRIATE?

When we are left to determine consequences, we have a limited range of repercussions that we can entertain educationally. We can offer revocation of recess, detention, and then, higher up the administrative line, suspend or expel.

The larger issue then becomes, however, does the "punishment fit the crime"? In other words, are we punishing a child or disciplining the student? What is the difference? Well, discipline is an educational function; in other words, we are attempting to teach the child something.

Think about this: Why do they call prisons "the department of corrections" and not "the department of bad behaviors"? Please know, this is not to make any comparison to a child with behavioral issues and a potential inmate. What we are saying is that in society the focus should be on corrective behaviors and discipline (versus simply and solely punishment).

WHAT IS THE DIFFERENCE BETWEEN PUNISHMENT AND DISCIPLINE?

• *Does it provide a "junior" example of a real-world consequence?*

  For instance, if a student is spending time goofing off in class versus doing his or her work, does it make sense that the student loses an entire recess?

  Well, let's take an adult example. Have you ever "goofed off" at work? Think back; it is almost a certainty that you have in perhaps the last week or so. The result? You have a reciprocal amount of work that you must do at some inopportune time (likely at home). For instance, thirty minutes of procrastination equals thirty minutes away from reality shows, talking to friends on the phone, or surfing social media during your off time.

Provide a "junior" example to your students in that thirty minutes of lack of focus from schoolwork provides an equivalent thirty minutes of work made up at once or in increments during time when they would rather be doing something else (i.e., recess, free time, at home, during activities).

- *Is this applied in a manner that is fair, firm, and consistent?*

  Let's go back to the example of getting pulled over for speeding. When the officer pulls you over, he is not generally angry. If he is truly doing his job (and you are doing yours as a citizen by pulling over immediately), he will speak in a calm, firm, and steady tone, and this professional interaction will follow.

  "License and registration, please?" You will provide this, and then a short exchange and the consequence will be rendered. Short, quick, calm, and precise. This is what you are striving to achieve in consequences with students as well.

  Being overly emotional, belaboring the issue with constant talking, empty threats, and/or nagging take away your efficiency and effectiveness. Less is more when it comes to application of a consequence.

- *Threats are not useful.*

  Going back to the home example, threats are often utilized with students in their household. "Don't do that. Don't do this or else!" Often, these are accompanied with extreme empty threats: "I will take away your cell phone for a month!" These threats take away a parent's effectiveness and, likewise, teach a child that he or she can often compromise his or her way out of an issue.

  When a child comes to school, he or she will test these boundaries. "Does no really mean no? Can I get away with this or that? They will give me several warnings before a consequence!"

  Think for a moment about the nature of this, however. Why do we give warnings? Generally, it is because we believe the student did not know better for what they were doing. So, in the case of a student with a behavioral issue, let's consider a few scenarios:

  o "Johnny, why did you hit him? This is your last warning!" (*Assumption: The student did not know better than punching a peer and needs a warning.*)
  o "Mary, why did you steal that pencil off my desk?" (*Assumption: Mary did not know stealing was wrong.*)

When you give warnings, you place a buffer in a student's understanding of cause and effect. In other words, "If I do this, then this happens." Think about when they are older adolescents on the brink of adulthood. "But, I stole this one item. Can I have a break with no consequences?" In some cases, that one behavior may be enough for an irrevocable consequence. Yet, in others, it will be, "Whew, I got away with that again!" No cause, no effect, no learning. It also teaches that you can attempt to talk your way out of an issue by distracting with details and smoothly talking your way out of a consequence versus facing up to it.

ARE STUDENTS TAUGHT TO STAND BY OR STAND UP?

On March 13, 1964, the most horrible example of what psychologists call the Bystander Effect occurred. Kitty Genovese was a hardworking young woman who was coming back from her night job in the wee hours in the morning in Queens, New York.

Following the path, she had followed so many times, a man by the name of Winston Moseley crossed her path. Later in interviews, Moseley noted he was seeking to "just kill a woman."

Moseley mercilessly attacked and stabbed her, over and over, while she screamed, "Oh my God! He stabbed me! Help me!" For well over thirty minutes, several neighbors reported hearing her screams but decided it was probably just an argument and went back to sleeping. One man finally shouted from his window, "Let that girl alone!" which scared Moseley away.

That witness most likely saw Kitty Genovese pulling her limp body across the street, under a streetlight, to her apartment yet did nothing to help her. Witnesses saw Moseley drive away, only to ten minutes later return, finding Kitty in the hallway at the rear of the building, where the door was locked and thus prevented her escape. He then continued to stab her to death over and over for another several minutes.

The next day the newspaper headlines blared, "Thirty-Eight Who Saw Murder Didn't Call Police." When the many who witnessed the matter, first-hand, were asked about their conduct in this situation, they said that they "just didn't want to get involved." A 911 call to the police may have saved her life, but each person either assumed someone else would do it, or it was simply best to not get involved.[3]

How does this relate to a school setting? Well, we have all heard the saying that "children can be cruel." Behaviors of a negative nature that gain attention in the educational setting are often done outside the careful and prolonged gaze of those adults in charge. When these behaviors are left unchecked, they spread. Further, it is impossible for educators to keep their eyes on every aspect of a pupil's day. Adults, additionally, are largely kept at a distance to the real pulse of what is going on in the social arena that is childhood.

If we are going to inoculate a school, we must train students to not support or encourage maladaptive behaviors. Curriculum must include testing ethical and situational dilemma and question why students choose to intervene or remain silent.

Therefore, encouraging students to assert themselves in conflict and bullying behavior patterns becomes a necessary strategy versus just focusing on the accused bully. How? Simply teaching all of our students assertiveness and conflict resolution skills is critical in this arena. Training children to speak out against poor or bullying behaviors avoids supporting these actions. Without such training? Children don't say anything (i.e., the Bystander Effect), encourage conflict, or even record negative actions for the viral audience of the empty pseudo-entertainment that is all too prevalent on certain parts of the Internet.

ALL STUDENTS MUST BE ENCOURAGED TO DO THE FOLLOWING:

- Distinguish between tattling and telling of an issue (i.e., is this an issue of bullying, harassment, intimidation, violence, or threats/dares?)
- Be rewarded and recognized for being assertive in situations that involve standing up for one's peers
- Parenting and student workshops on being a good digital citizen as well as how to avoid the scourge that is cyberbullying

Coordination of law enforcement, child services, and mental health agencies must be encouraged to provide a blanket of service communication and collaboration. Keep in mind that a fair amount of the students with behavioral issues will likely have touched one, or more, of these organizations.

SURVEYING SCHOOL CLIMATE

As school climate disintegrates, behaviors conversely ramp up. Anonymously surveying teachers, students, and parents allows us to gauge the temperature of the school climate. A climate that is warm allows for better behavior, while one that is cold exacerbates harsh behaviors. (See appendix.)

EDUCATION IS ABOUT CHARACTER

Five decades ago, Dr. Martin Luther King Jr. prophesied the importance of intertwining character and public education when he said, "We must remember that intelligence is not enough. Intelligence plus character—that is the goal of true education. The complete education gives one not only power of concentration, but worthy objectives upon which to concentrate."

That being said, with the role of educating comes the dual responsibility of teaching character. There are plenty of intelligent people, who wilt in the face of being able to contribute to society in a positive manner. Although initially they may succeed based on sheer ability, the lack of character ultimately leads to their undoing in the society around them. Character is incubated in childhood and is like a sharpened tool that is used/applied in public education.

When we discuss character, we must consider such important and time-honored concepts as being trustworthy, responsible, fair, caring, and being a good citizen of one's school and world.

RESPONSIBILITY IS BECOMING AN ENDANGERED SPECIES

Children are becoming less and less responsible for their actions and their behaviors. It is quite obvious when a child triangulates parents and educators about grades, attendance, or behavior and then watches the fireworks fly (as he or she chuckles quietly in the corner). These scenarios reinforce a child's belief that gaining negative adult attention trumps responsibility for one's actions.

Further, if a child does not witness adults taking responsibility and sees adults always pointing the proverbial finger at one another, he or she will likely emulate this behavior on his or her own. Taking responsibility is easy when you get a good grade and can post it on the fridge. Far harder is the grade that you earned when you did not work and must equally declare responsibility regardless of the fragile ego that many of our youth now exhibit.

THE MARSHMALLOW EXPERIMENT ON RESPONSIBILITY, NOT JUST FLUFF

In the 1970s, psychologist Walter Mischel at Stanford University conducted a series of experiments.[4] The concept of the study was simple, in that a child was offered a choice between one marshmallow now and two marshmallows if he or she waited until the researcher returned. The researcher would then leave the room for fifteen minutes, and when he or she came back (if the marshmallow was still intact), the child would now receive two marshmallows as a reward for their patience in waiting. How does this correlate to behavioral issues with pupils?

The children of this investigation were followed into adulthood, and it was determined that those who were able to take the responsibility of disciplining themselves and wait for the two marshmallows had superior SAT scores, higher rates of educational success as adults, as well as several other attributes necessary for lifetime success.[5] The bottom line is the younger a child can establish responsibility and self-discipline for himself or herself, the better a chance to sculpt success as an adult. Thus, the earlier we can reach children in school, the more opportunity we have to shape our future generation's destiny.

THE GOLDEN RULE OF RESPONSIBILITY

When we do anything that our child(ren)/students can do for themselves, we effectively disable them. The subtle, unwarranted message that we are giving them is, "You are not capable of doing this on your own; you need adult help." This leads, in turn, to self-esteem problems and/or overreliance on others.

As Henry Ford once said, "If you think you can do a thing or think you can't do a thing, you're right." In terms of teaching or parenting if you tell a child directly or subtly that he or she can't do something, "you're right." Take the case of a child trying his or her best to do a task, and you do not like the way he or she is doing it. Abruptly you discount what the child did and change it to the way *you* think is correct. The message is *you* failed or are not good enough.

Ask the child to try the same, or similar, task later, and he or she doesn't seem motivated or try at all. We now say, "See, they are unmotivated." From the child's perspective they say, "Why, bother? They are just going to change or correct it anyway. I can't do it right." We have taught them the concept of "learned helplessness"—a psychological term for, quite simply put, learning laziness or throwing in the towel that is more effective than trying.

A CHILD WHO CAN'T TRUST ONE'S ENVIRONMENT

When we discuss issues of trustworthiness, we are addressing how much we can trust and believe that students will do what they say they are going to do. Further, we are able to know that their educational community can count on them, as can their peers, teachers, and other vital members in their lives.

For some of our children, due to their chaotic family lives, they do not inherently trust anyone as a necessary and vital survival skill. What should be a foundational requirement of childhood, that of a trusted adult and home life, is not readily provided. So, a child's knee-jerk reaction is to attack and/or test the boundaries of his or her respective environments to see how adults may react to a child's initial maladaptive behaviors.

Therefore, the primary means by which we can teach students trust is by establishing an environment that fosters trust. Physical and emotional safety is key. Can the child feel free of bullying? Can the child feel safe from harm and be able to express himself or herself without the harsh spotlight of criticism or ridicule? Is the classroom routine regular and predictable? Do educators and the educational system follow through with what is being promised, or, alternatively, are promises empty and only sporadically fulfilled? Remember that many children with bad home lives have had promises broken time and time again. It is their proactive strategy to anticipate that the world is one of chaos, constant change, and eventual disappointment.

UNDERSTANDING BEFORE CARING

In the earliest stages of a child's development, the child has to be egocentric. The child is not able to care for own in any way. Therefore, the world revolves around the child with adults caring, feeding, and changing him or her. The adult world orbits around the child like planets in their ever eating, wetting, and crying little universe. In turn, the infant learns that the world truly is "all about me."

As children get into primary and the start of elementary school, they continue this self-centered concept in their interactions. They look at the world and believe that they are the cause of all that happens in their universe, a term commonly referred to as "magical thinking." In reality, they have little control regarding what goes on around them.

As they become older, they must learn to shift that concept of "self-centeredness" to one of "other centeredness"—namely, the notion of empathy, the first foundational step to caring for others. The first test of this focus away from self is, in fact, the educational system. Therefore, caring must be fostered at school if we are going to have any hope for future generations to develop a better world than our own.

Children tend to try everything they can to seek adult approval. Hence, when you are watching them, they will do what they need to do to demonstrate such approval. That being said, you will be a proverbial "fly on the wall" when you get the accurate barometer of what is *truly* going on in the children's peer societal climate. Therefore, just listening and "catching children being good" is an often overused but vital technique. However, it is effective if it is done without student awareness that they are being monitored or recognized for it accordingly. Only then you can get an accurate gauge of a child's true motives and behaviors.

Caring starts from the top down in schools. If the administration is apathetic, so is the faculty, and (exponentially) so are the pupils.

THE ATTITUDE OF GRATITUDE

In a world that is ever increasingly more frenetic and hurried, we forget to often let those around us know what we are grateful for. We make an assumption (or hope) that those who surround us know that we appreciate what they do on a daily basis. The notion is that gratefulness and care, however, have become lost in the sauce of our world that has little time for such banal pleasantries.

How important is gratitude in the motivation of education? A recent study by Glassdoor, an employment company, found that 88 percent of employees state that they would work more diligently for an appreciative boss. Further, of those, 70 percent note that they would feel better about the work they do if the boss appreciated them on a regular basis.[6] Think then how vitally important is that concept in the educational workplace for each and every person, an impressionable youth comes in contact with?

Give opportunities to display gratefulness whenever and wherever you can. Create bulletin boards, use handwritten notes, and address achievements on the school's website.

The point being, make certain that your fellow faculty members and students feel that thankfulness and voice gratitude for each other. Make them that "70–88 percent" who feel better and work harder because of the feeling of acceptance and appreciation by educators and within the school community.

FEELING A PART OF YOUR SCHOOL—CITIZENSHIP

Why do children join gangs? The short answer, via most research, is, simplistically, to belong. The youth have an inherent desire to be part of something bigger than themselves. In short, when a family structure is lacking, children will fill the void with something, anything, to feel as though they have some type of attachment: sense of belonging.

This basic psychological need is exploited among most gangs via their numerous initiations and rituals. As confirmation of the success of this strategy, to date, "There are approximately, 24,500 known youth gangs with about 772,500 youth members. That's about 7% of the US's teen population," according to an article published in *Psychology Today* by Raychelle Cassada Lohmann (MS, LPCS).[7]

Clearly, not every child will join a gang; however, children may bond with others who are a bad influence and still will lead them down a very wrong path of life. Though not a gang, it is the parallel sense that they have a peer group that steers them in the direction of potential misdeeds or, more succinctly known as, "hanging out with the wrong crowd."

Yet, in direct contrast to this issue is a classroom and a public school that represent the brightest best hope for a child to feel a part of something even larger. In no other place will children have the opportunity to meet a larger community of their peers under one roof than that of the public school environment. So the question is, how do we make them feel an esteemed citizen of their school system?

We must start by the following:

- Providing a safe place that allows for all types of students and dialogue without fear of reprisal or negative criticism.
- A school that stands up and fosters students who are different in culture, ethnicity, sexual orientation, disability, and viewpoints and that fosters productive, nonthreatening dialogue in these areas.
- Schools that provide extracurricular activities that meet the greatest scope of interests and idiosyncratic interests (e.g., Legos, technology, and other areas that are outside of the mainstream).
- A strong and consistent antibullying and character education curriculum infused within the school system-wide.
- Parental programs that support the recognition of the school district as a community-wide entity and allow for community events.
- A front-office staff that is welcoming. Remember that a first impression is vital in a school. If your front-office staff is not welcoming to students and parents, this puts a negative face to all who arrive and sets the tone for one's view of the school in general.
- Allow for volunteering; having volunteers (who are properly selected) provides for a community-based, welcoming atmosphere.
- Offer opportunities for the students to see other community agencies that they can become involved with by opening invitations up to these organizations to collaborate with the school and its staff (provided this can be done safely).
- Invite parents for events by pairing the parent program with student-based activities.
- Everyone (from custodian to administrator) should be welcoming to students, parents, and everyone who arrive to the building. For a good parallel of this, think of the best customer service example: Disney. According to Disneyfantic.com, "[Employees] are trained to the highest efficacy and they all have one thing in mind: to make the guests happy. You will see many cast members (workers) go above and beyond to meet your needs and to exceed your expectations. . . . [from every worker] . . . you are sure to experience top-notch quality service."[8]

- Allow for anonymous suggestions: A suggestion box helps for the entire community to offer ideas on how to make the school even more friendly and welcoming.
- Offer family nights: Whether it be a family game night, a family literacy night, or a family movie night, respect the importance of the family dynamic being fully embraced and recognized into the school dynamic. Consider asking parent–teacher association/parent–teacher organization (PTA/PTO) for food or having the PTA/PTO offer free advertising in exchange for a local restaurant's donation of food/snacks (if cost is a concern).
- Allow for marketing: having pep rallies, stickers, shirts, and bulletin boards that taut your school spirit helps to spread the word systematically through the school and the community.

RECOGNIZING ALL DISABILITIES

In our schools we tend to diligently recognize learning and physical disabilities. We tailor our instruction to children who have difficulty with math and reading. We have handicap-accessible facilities so that those with physical issues can have the full school experience.

Students who have significant behavioral issues, in many senses, are disabled from gaining the full educational experience as well. They are often handicapped from social relationships, and the frustration that they feel in many areas keeps them from academically blooming to their full potential as well. Parents speak ill of them, students segregate them, and even (sometimes) they become the topic of harsh criticism in the faculty room.

Therefore, as we modify and adapt academics to other limitations of our pupils, one must consider tailoring to the behavioral constraints of our students as well. That is not to say make excuses for behaviors. Rather, it is to say that behavior also places a barrier to a student's success just as any other limitation. Therefore, classrooms would benefit from adjusting to these disabilities of all of our children.

APPRECIATING LEARNING STYLES

Think about when you were in school. How did your teachers teach?

Often, teachers tended to lecture for prolonged periods at the board and students would raise their hands, ask questions, and engage in reciprocal auditory dialog. When teachers wanted to "mix things up a bit," they tended to use visual cues or reminders to attempt cementing further the curricula being taught.

In a web article by Shannon Hutton for the website Education.com, she noted that "these kids (those with behaviors) were considered hyperactive and difficult. Now we know better. These students aren't being difficult. They just learn differently."[9] In fact, most students with behavioral issues tend to learn from a kinesthetic learning style, that is, in the touching and experiencing.

Yet, as educators we tend to fall back into the comfortable cradle of an auditory learning perspective primarily, followed by a visual paradigm, and lastly, kinesthetic, which requires the most planning and time. Unfortunately, that order is generally the exact opposite to the strengths of those students with behavioral issues. A school and classroom, hence, must work to the learning style of all students.

INCONSISTENT STAFFING

Working with a child with behavioral issues can be extraordinarily difficult. Many times these students are oppositional and defiant and can otherwise be a great challenge to handle. Therefore, they may not be the "favorite" of some educators. Hence, they are shuffled from classroom to classroom or teachers who are novices and are given the classroom of these students as a "rite of passage." The seasoned teachers who would best be able to assist them are needed whenever possible; this is just as those with significant educational challenges are in need of the most adept instructors as well.

A school must make certain with challenging students that the teacher indeed wants to work with this population. Generally, that is a teacher who is firm, consistent, respectful of the students, and not easily rattled and has a sense of humor. Those who have the skills and patience to teach these students also will reap the benefits of their hard work. Not to mention, if you do not provide the right environment for these pupils, they will monopolize the time of many more than just the one or two teachers within the classroom.

SUSPENDING SUSPENSIONS

Think about a student who is not attending school. He has few rules, consequences, or boundaries at home aside from what video game to play and not bothering his parents. He lives in an all-inclusive vacation of limitless food, video games, sleep, and social media. No rules, no expectations.

Now, he has to go to a school that involves getting up early, doing work, waiting to eat lunch, and no social media for an extended period. Why on earth would he want this choice? So, he goes to school and gets suspended due to his behavior—three more days of an all-inclusive vacation! Next time, he will have to try harder or increase his behavior for a better chance to get back to his personal vacation resort.

CLUB MOM AND DAD

Another example of a child who chooses to try to get home is far sadder. The student knows that his or her mother is depressed/sick/substance abusing. Leaving his or her parent brings a great deal of guilt and confusion. The thought occurs, "Perhaps if I tantrum, I will get a chance to stay home and care for my mother who really needs me."

Suspensions, therefore, must be an internal manner of discipline. In-school suspensions keep the student "in school." It reinforces the fact that consequences in school are handled in school, where rules and consequences can best be handled and remedied for educational matters.

NOTES

1. Ed Fuller, "Examining Principal Turnover," Shanker Institute, July 16, 2012, www.shankerinstitute.org/blog/examining-principal-turnover.

2. Eric Mosley, "4 Reasons Employee Appreciation Matters Year-Round," *Huffington Post*, March 3, 2016, www.huffingtonpost.com/eric-mosley/4-reasons-employee-apprec_b_9368584.html.

3. Harold Takooshian, "The 1964 Kitty Genovese Tragedy: What Have We Learned?" *Psychology Today*, Sussex Publishers, March 24, 2014.

4. Walter Mischel, Robert Zeiss, and Antonette Zeiss, "Stanford Preschool Internal-External Scale," *PsycTESTS Dataset*, 1974, doi: 10.1037/t05737-000.

5. Walter Mischel, Robert Zeiss, and Antonette Zeiss, "Stanford Preschool Internal-External Scale," *PsycTESTS Dataset*, 1974, doi: 10.1037/t05737-000.

6. Varuni Khosla, "88% Employees Willing to Stay Longer If Appreciated at Work: Survey," *Economic Times*, November 2, 2016, economictimes.india-times.com/jobs/88-employees-willing-to-stay-longer-if-appreciated-at-work-survey/articleshow/55202176.cms.

7. Raychelle Cassada Lohmann, "Teen Gangstas," *Psychology Today*, Sussex Publishers, October 11, 2010, www.psychologytoday.com/blog/teen-angst/201010/teen-gangstas.

8. "Disney Lists Archives," DisneyFanatic.com, www.disneyfanatic.com/category/disney-lists/.

9. "Helping Auditory Learners Succeed," Education.com, September 16, 2013, www.bing.com/cr?IG=75DC3C22F1B24F7C96214BD208B7E36F&CID=045EB6 3607D76D1A0C88BD9B06786CE0&rd=1&h=hTjW_4G5lVJrj8lJZAX7IzHtNCe 3_z_CbYnxQ_QEZBU&v=1&r=https%3a%2f%2fwww.education.com%2fmagazin e%2farticle%2fauditory_learners%2f&p=DevEx,5072.1.

Chapter 4

The Teacher

That's You . . . You Are the One Who Makes It All Work!

The mediocre teacher tells. The good teacher explains. The superior teacher demonstrates. The great teacher inspires.

—William Arthur Ward

As you turn on the bright fluorescent lights, you realize that these neatly stacked rows of desks and the whiteboard are yours for the next ten months. You realize that this is your classroom, the place where children will be entrusted in your care, the place where you will be responsible for teaching them academics and social skills that they will carry with them for the rest of their lives. You will be the one with whom they spend more time with than anyone else.

That reality is suddenly both frightening and exhilarating. You think to yourself, "How will I make a difference in their lives? What will they think of me? What will their parents think of me? Can I control this class? What if they know how nervous I am? Can I do this?"

Your thoughts are suddenly interrupted by the sharp shrill of a classroom bell. It is too late to turn back now. Students stream into your classroom, chattering and laughing about the memories of the summer that are now evaporating like the morning dew in the beginnings of the crisp autumn air.

For a moment you want to run out of the classroom and hide, but it is too late. You suddenly have twenty-five pairs of eyes staring at you. Wondering, pondering, "What will you teach me? Will you care about me? Respect me? Help me?" Yes, it is too late to run, far too late.

BEING A BAD REFLECTION

Watch at your local box department store and you will see it: the bad mirrors—parents who entertain a youth temper tantrum with an adult temper tantrum of their own. The parallels are all there: the stomping, the screaming, the pleading, and (sometimes) even the crying. The parents reflect back what they see whether they recognize it or not. In turn, they get back what they give. It is a self-fulfilling behavioral loop.

As an educator, we sometimes, without realizing it, also entertain and feed that reactive loop with our students through empty words and/or reactive emotions. At its worst, it leads to a string of escalating empty threats that we cannot, or will not, follow through with. This is also better known as the "classic power struggle."

It goes something like this:

Student: "I am not doing this f**ing work! This sucks!"

Educator: "Now settle down. We will not have that kind of talk in this class!"

Student: "This is too f*in hard! I am not doing it!"

Educator: "That's it. You now have a recess detention!"

Student: "F**k that!"

Educator: "I said that's enough! I don't know who you think you are talking to!"

Student: (He now breaks a pencil and rips up his paper.) "This class sucks!"

Educator: "That's it. Now you have an after-school detention!"

Student: "What the f**k! F**k you!"

Let's take a look at this interaction from a different vantage point. First, the educator missed a very key aspect of the interaction: the student was struggling with frustration and anticipatory anxiety of the classwork itself. When both of them began experiencing anger, both entered into the trap of tunnel vision—that is, the educator focused on profanity, punishment, and anger. The student was focused on frustration, lack of perceived fairness, and anger as well. During this time, neither could focus on anything else but getting their point across to the other.

If you have ever been cut off on the highway and used your choice of profanities as well as some inappropriate gestures, you get what this is like. The ideal would be to continue to steer safely, drive at a reasonable speed, and avoid the possibility of engaging in the ever-increasing statistics of a potential violent road rage incident. Yet, your brain is hijacked and "tunnel visioned" toward the perpetrator who caused you the potential of a possible motor vehicle accident.

You have no clue that the line of profane language, the outrageous speed you travel to catch up with "that idiot," or the fact that your impressionable child is in the car seems to matter one bit in your handling of this issue.

DON'T MAKE STATEMENT QUESTIONS

When you want a student to do something, don't make a command a question. When you tell a student who is strong-willed, "Would you please sit over there?" Or, if you ask a pupil, "Sit over here, okay?" You're asking, not telling. In our adult-oriented world, we soften commands couched in the form of a question so as not to seem rude or offensive.

Difficulty is when you make the same statement to a student who tends to be more concrete and does not have the formalities that are present in the adult world, those passive requests are deemed as questions where the student then perceives that he or she has a choice. The educator then receives the honest answer which is, "No I don't want to sit there. No it is not 'okay' that you want me to do this."

If you have a command, do so politely, but make it specific and direct. For instance:

Instead of: "Can you sit over there?"
Try: "Please sit in the red chair at this table."
Instead of: "I need you to go get your homework please, okay?"
Try: "Please get your homework out of your backpack and place it in the bin at the back table."

There are two subtle differences between the two contrasting educator's statements: The first ones are questions and the second are commands. In addition, the second are more specific than the generalized statements made in the first inquiries.

LET THE BUCK STOP WITH YOU . . . WHEN POSSIBLE!

President Harry S. Truman had a saying that he coined and had sitting on his desk in the Oval Office: "The buck stops here." He embodied this quote as a mission of statement of sorts because he knew, as president, he was ultimately responsible for whatever came across his desk and he could not defer to any other authority who was higher than his own.

As educators, we must (again) keep in mind that students are in a constant need to seek some control of the domains of their life. Remember, as we noted earlier in this book, adults control ultimately everything; they inherently know you are the boss (or should be aware of that fact).

When you seek to gain control with a poor customer service interaction, what do you do? Generally, we ask to speak to "the manager" thinking that the person has more authority and therefore can put us on a level playing field with the particular airline, cable provider, or cell phone carrier. Correct? We don't let "the buck" stop in the lap of the unhelpful frontline customer service representative.

When you send a child to an administrator, (if you are not one) you have essentially said, "I am sorry young, belligerent customer. I am helpless to assist you in this matter. Please let me have you speak to my supervisor immediately." It is as if you have put the controls right in the lap of the student.

Now, of course, there are times that you must involve an administrator each and every time:

- Threats of physical harm to self or others
- Destruction of property
- Bullying (depends on state law whom these get reported to)

However, other issues should be handled at the lowest level of the chain of command—that is, you as a teacher or if it comes to you as an administrator. How do you feel when an irate parent attempts to usurp respect and gain control by going "right to the top"? Likely, you feel irritated that they did not attempt to engage the situation at your level first; don't give the child that message inadvertently by your actions.

DO NOT QUESTION WHAT YOU KNOW OR SEE

Let's imagine a child comes from a very punitive home, where everything is dealt with punishment and there is "a use to crying over spilled milk." When that child, hence, spills milk in a rush to finish breakfast, he or she is scared. The parent asks, "Did you spill that milk?" That question is a classic—what psychologists call "a double bind." That is, you are darned if you do and darned if you don't. If you say yes, punishment. Say no? Punishment for lying. It is more commonly known as a "lose/lose situation."

It can be applied to the school environment as well. If you absolutely know a child cheated, stole, spilled, hit, or broke something, don't ask if he or she did it. You are setting up the very same context.

If you are certain the child did it, say it, address it, and move on. Don't play a guessing game. Or, can I catch them in a lie? It is a losing proposition for all involved, and you lose a part of your authority in an unneeded power struggle.

MAKING THE MISTAKE THAT THE QUIET ONES ALWAYS ARE BEST ADJUSTED

Think about who gets the majority of your attention? Is it the majority of students neatly in a row, with their nose to the proverbial grindstone dutifully whittling away at paper after paper, assignment after assignment? Is it those who raise their hands eager to answer the next question that drops from your lips?

No, our attention is focused on the child who flips over that desk, who curses out the unfair nature of school, and who breaks that pencil and, in turn, our will. It is that student whom every student and faculty member from administrator to custodian know by name and face—those who earn a reputation and are burned into the memory of everyone as a disciplinary legend for years to come.

But what about the student who turns that anger inward? Who holds it in like a shaken soda bottle that ceases to let the fainted wisps of anger out? The one who is always the wallflower, the outsider, the square peg in the constant round hole of academic life? Their behavior is just as destructive, if not more so than the child who flips a desk. You just don't see it churning and raging just below the seemingly calm surface is a rip tide of potentially epic proportions.

Yet, it behooves you to see these students too. Some of these students make it to adulthood, scarred but surviving. Others take that anger and destroy themselves via drugs, alcohol, sex, or suicide. Others explode when the waves crash above the surface and attack others in a single explosive fit that no one expected.

In our recognition of this, we must realize that behaviors both positive and maladaptive cannot merely be "pigeonholed" into one stereotyped aspect or another. Labels are for jars and not students, and all student behaviors must be recognized by looking at the following:

- Character education curriculum must be interwoven within the educational fabric of a school. Doing so enhances the climate of such important and needed skills such as caring, empathy, trustworthiness, and responsibility. Character education, however, is not merely an assembly or a single activity. It must be celebrated and spliced into every aspect of the school day and climate. Not just a "one trick pony" to say, "We checked that off the list."
- Students who are more anxiety-ridden will be less likely to verbalize concerns, needs, or wants. In turn, they will keep worries and fears under wraps and let them eat them up inside. Consider an alternate means of communicating concerns such as an anonymous suggestion/concern box that they

can quietly drop a note (or draw) these concerns. These students you will want to address one-on-one, out of the earshot of their peers.
- Students who are overly passive must be taught assertiveness and conflict resolution skills (more on this later). Some children are naturally more aggressive, others are more passive, and some are inclined to be more extroverted while others the inverse. Each style, however, has its significant benefits and some drawbacks, which creates issues for either of these students on the extreme sides of the spectrum. (See figure 4.1.)

It is our obligation, indeed our ethical duty, to know and scratch just beneath that fragile facade to see what is beneath it. Those who are passive or on the periphery will not show you that piece of themselves, unless you ask and carefully dig for it.

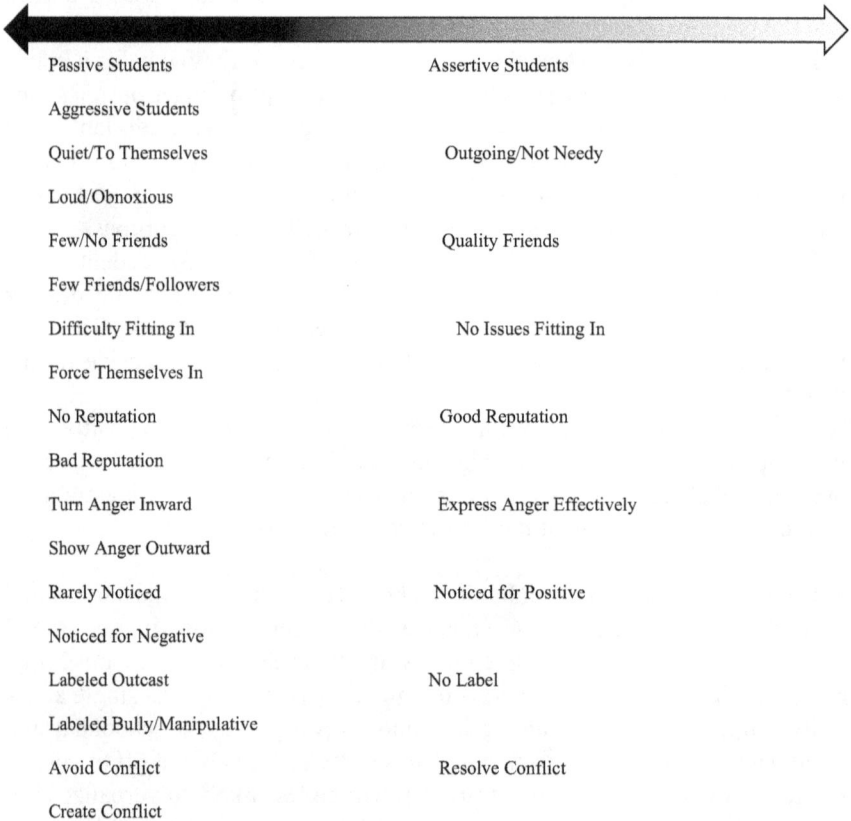

Passive Students	Assertive Students
Aggressive Students	
Quiet/To Themselves	Outgoing/Not Needy
Loud/Obnoxious	
Few/No Friends	Quality Friends
Few Friends/Followers	
Difficulty Fitting In	No Issues Fitting In
Force Themselves In	
No Reputation	Good Reputation
Bad Reputation	
Turn Anger Inward	Express Anger Effectively
Show Anger Outward	
Rarely Noticed	Noticed for Positive
Noticed for Negative	
Labeled Outcast	No Label
Labeled Bully/Manipulative	
Avoid Conflict	Resolve Conflict
Create Conflict	

Figure 4.1. Student Behaviors Run the Spectrum

AVOID GETTING BOGGED IN TOO MUCH DETAIL

If you involve in too much detail in a prospective consequence that you wish to employ, it creates confusion. If you cannot explain a consequence in a simple sentence or two, do not apply it. In addition, make certain that the consequence is concrete in nature, simple, effective, and age-appropriate.

Remember that children with behavioral issues tend to be more concrete in their thinking versus their peers. They also tend to not question too much extraneous detail that might be involved in a consequence. One may say that this is manipulative in nature, and it can be an inability to understand beyond a limited scope of understanding. Either way, the response still works the same. Less is more and simpler is better.

- *Consequence too complicated:* "If you don't do your math work now, you will have to miss recess tomorrow and I will have to contact your mom. You will also have to take your clip and alter it on the chart."
- *Consequence with less detail:* "Since you talked during math, you will miss fifty minutes of recess."

BE WARY OF CONSEQUENCES THAT HAVE NO TEETH

Sometimes, we attempt to utilize parents as a stakeholder for consequences in the school domain. Keep in mind that what parents have shown you in their past actions (i.e., not returning calls, not picking up a student when you call to do so), they are likely to do the same in the future. This may seem like common sense; however, how many times do we continue to try to use the parent as a support, only to be proverbially "stood up" each time?

Therefore, calling these parents to address a consequence is akin to an empty threat. Provide consequences that are adequate at school as well as reward systems. This will allow you to provide an "internal reward/consequence system" that will be far more effective for the student and school setting alike.

- *Consequence with no teeth:* "We are going to call your father and he is not going to be happy" (despite the fact that the parent has done nothing to indicate involvement or concern).
- *Consequence with teeth:* "Due to your behavior, you are going to stay after school tomorrow to do the work that you did not do today because of your behavior and you will take the late bus home" (internal consequence—no parental involvement needed).

"GIVING PIZZA WHEN I WANT A HAMBURGER"

Let's think about the thought process for most children; they do not focus about any one thing for a significant length of time. This, in recent years, has been amplified by the fact that in our Internet-connected world and a world has created seemingly limitless choices. Think of how many more choices you have when you go to the grocery store. Think of how much information you have at your fingertips from your smartphone.

This data has led to a virtual rewiring of our students' brains. They do not focus on any item for even a miniscule length of time anymore because the world is simply showering down so much information. Technology has rewired all our brains. Need an example? Can you remember the top five numbers of your contacts on your cell phone? Can you read a map?

These were survival skills and expectations that we all had only a few years ago. Now, we have rewired ourselves because cell phones and GPS have eliminated the need for those skills. A few simple swipes of a smartphone screen have taken the place of these more complex tasks.

Why is this important? Because children are much the same way. They become bored easily by anything that is not dynamic, challenging, or fluidly changing. If you were told you could have your most favorite food in an end-less supply, you may initially be excited. If you were told that was all you could eat for breakfast, lunch, and dinner, you would likely quickly become bored and agitated as this was now your only singular option.

So it is with students; change your rewards frequently and often. Doing so will keep students "on their toes," not knowing the rewards that they will get and avoid boredom. Before you deal with behaviors, however, you must establish rewards ahead of time. Some educators attempt to establish a reward in the throes of a behavior. Doing so is a recipe for failure as a child will generally be oppositional during these junctures and likely to tell what he or she doesn't want versus what he or she doesn't need.

Remember, positive interventions are always a better alternative to nega-tive. Having a student work toward something, instead of avoiding a potential consequence, helps avoid the cycle of a child learning that negative behaviors provide more attention than positive responses. From an adult perspective, you work *for* a paycheck, not to *avoid* being evicted or foreclosed upon.

DON'T PAINT YOURSELF INTO A CORNER

Often, in family settings, parents find themselves painted into a proverbial "corner." They take "everything" away, the proverbial childhood, equivalent of a life sentence. Next, the child does something wrong and the parent has nothing left to take away. Now, anything that is promised to be done is merely an empty threat.

Similarly, this occurs when a teacher only has negative consequences. Quickly, the number of consequences that you have at your disposal evaporates and you are left throwing up your hands with few or no options left.

The following (see table 4.1) are a means of expanding the number of positive rewards that you can utilize.

Table 4.1. Reinforcement Inventory

If you could do something with your teacher, name three things you would like to do.
If you could do an activity with three students, who would they be?
If you were principal for the day, what three things would you change in school?
If you could do any activity at recess, what would be your top three choices?
If you could do something with the free time in class, what are the three things you would choose?
If you could take out three books/videos from the school library, what would they be?
If you could play three educational apps on the computer or tablet at school, which ones would you choose?
If you could eat lunch with three people at school, who would they be?
If you could have three rewards in school, what would you want to have?

APPLYING REINFORCEMENT REWARDS

Oftentimes, educators, and parents for that matter, are stymied when they realize that "nothing seems to work" in regard to reinforcements, rewards, or behavior contracts with a particular child. The adults are then often stuck asking themselves, "Well, it worked for a while but then the effectiveness seemed to stop." It is as if the child's motivation has suddenly evaporated and left the educators in a steamy haze of frustration.

DON'T OFFER THE BIG-SCREEN TELEVISION FIRST

Children, like any of us, work on a hierarchy system. We want as much as we can for the least amount of effort possible. Further, the majority of us hate to settle if we know we can get a better deal if we "wait it out."

Therefore, it is imperative with the reward system you utilize that it is tiered to be certain, you offer the smallest reward(s) possible that is effective. Once you raise the bar higher, you can never go back as the student simply will not accept such a compromise.

RESPECT IS KEY

Often, we expect respect from our students. They should respect us because "we are the educators and they are the students." So goes the power struggle of "I (the educator) won't budge and give respect, until I get respect." The students dig their heels in and say, "Who do those teachers think they are? We are not going to respect them because they don't respect us." And so, the game of Chicken continues with neither party budging in this tug of war of a childish power struggle.

Let's look at this from a different perspective. Our job is to "teach" students and educate them on what it will take to be successful adults. Part of teaching is modeling. What if a child has never had to respect an adult, that child had never been respected, or just has no idea what the concept is like? It takes the adult to teach and model the concept of respect first. Take a quick informal survey of middle school students, and you may likely find that "being respected" is one of the top attributes of what this particular student population wants in a teacher. It is likely that elementary students would say the same thing if they could eloquently voice such thoughts.

THE JADED EDUCATOR

In the current world of education, it can become far too easy to become jaded, pointing the finger at the parents, the school, the administration, and others. The difficulty becomes when you point fingers toward others and obstacles, you lose focus on what you can indeed control and alter.

If you focus continually on what is within your locus of control, it will expand. Constantly, stepping out of your locus of control and your abilities will cause it to shrink and wither. In short, you become jaded. (See table 4.2.)

Table 4.2. Trait Inside/Outside Your Locus of Control

What Is within Your Control?	What Is outside Your Control?
Your attitude	Others' attitudes
Your continued professional development	Others' professionalism
How you interact with the students	How students relate to you
How you relate with your peers	How coworkers relate to you
Your priorities	The priorities of the school
Caring for yourself	School politics/gossip
Your actions	The actions of the school/district

SAY "YES" WHENEVER POSSIBLE

It is preferable to have a student who worked toward something versus restricting rewards or benefits. Students will always work and be more motivated by working toward versus away from something (as we discussed briefly previously in this chapter). Remember the parallel to adult behavior; most of us think we are working to "gain a paycheck and money" versus "to avoid being evicted."

Most of us tend to work toward something versus away from a consequence. Therefore, first determine your rewards and use them before scraping the "bottom of the barrel" for consequences or punitive actions.

"DO . . . DO" VERSUS "DON'T . . . DON'T"

How many times as an educator do you find yourself saying, "Don't do this. . . don't do that"? Often, we make the relatively far-reaching assumption that the children know *what* you expect them to do. For example, suppose someone had told you not to sit in the seat you were sitting in? You may promptly stand up, and then they tell you, with an annoyed tone, not to stand up. In frustration, you plop yourself back down on the seat. Now, they irritably tell you, "I SAID not to sit down."

What do you do next? You cannot and do not know what to do because you were not given actual directions; you simply were given restrictions that the speaker had assumed were directive in nature. They were not useful to the child who does not know what are the alternatives (as they are only tacitly assumed).

ASSUMING GREATER REWARD EQUATES TO GREATER SUCCESS ALWAYS

Think about your dream job; it could be a professional football player, an airline pilot, musician, doctor, actor/actress, or teacher, of course, whatever your heart desires. Now, do you have the physical prowess and size to be a pro football player? The cool-headedness to be a pilot in an emergency, the ability to pass the rigors of medical school, the voice of an angel for singing, or the luck to get your "big break "in the cut-throat world of Hollywood"?

- If you said "no," it may be because you know your skill set, musical voice that should be saved only for singing in the shower, or average physical abilities. These attributes helped bend you toward a similar career choice.

One could "sweeten the deal" toward your getting that dream occupation you want. These could come in the form of huge checks, bonuses, untold fame benefits, and the world on a platter that you still don't recognize your limits. No matter what they offer, you still have your abilities and idiosyncratic strengths and weaknesses. Are you being oppositional, defiant, manipulative? No, you are being realistic in understanding your limitations.

So, why do we assume then that a student who is not doing what we asked is being equally manipulative, defiant, or noncompliant? Could it be that the student simply lacks the capabilities to reach the reward or task we have laid in front of him or her? It doesn't matter the size of the carrot if the child lacks the teeth to "chew on" what is being offered.

THE SELF-FULFILLING PROPHECY

When you label a child (either in your head or in your communication), could it be that you are setting the stage for a self-fulfilling prophecy? What does this specifically mean? Put quite simply, students will perform toward your expectations.

If those expectations are of a negative nature, negative behaviors will incite negative reactions. Not certain of this? Think about how a kindergarten student who hangs on your every word for approval. Fact is, you can get them to agree or disagree with what you are saying, if they think this is the answer you want to hear. You are, in effect, establishing a "self-fulfilling prophecy" by getting them to respond how you want. The better question is, however, are they learning or parroting?

Here are three examples of potential self-fulfilling prophecies:

- "You had better not (fill in the behavioral blank) or I will have to . . . "
- "I hope now that you have returned to the class you won't (name the behavior of your choice)."
- "He/she is the one who *always* is (name the behavior of note)."

They all have in common that they do not tell the student what to do but challenge, and indeed may even encourage, the student to misbehave.

ACCLIMATIZE THE FISH SLOWLY

When you purchase a saltwater fish from a pet store, you must do two things to assure its survival: (1) spend a few hours carefully, drop by drop, adding water from your tank into the bag of water from the plastic bag the fish is in, to assure its survival with the transition in water conditions and (2) shut off all the lights in the aquarium and feverishly overfeed the fish in the other part of the tank so they don't attack and attempt to kill their new roommate.

How does this apply to the class setting? When a child returns to your classroom because of having a behavioral issue or significant change in routine, all eyes are on him or her. Let them slip in quietly. Don't acknowledge the incident that occurred or allow all eyes to be directed on them. Doing so provides either anxiety or an audience. Neither of these elements is good in fostering behavior that is not maladaptive in nature.

ANXIETY: THE ROOT OF MANY BEHAVIORS

Ever been on a roller coaster? Some of us enjoy the thrill of the dips and dives, twists and turns. Others find the same sensation utterly terrifying and will cause a person to cry, curse, and, in some cases, become violent with fear and angst. Yet others will shut down completely as the circuitry of our brain is tripped by an overload of fright.

So it is with children who have anxiety issues, which are often mislabeled as mere anger, spite, or manipulation. It is generally acknowledged that children with so-called behavior disorders are poor at self-reflection and reading their own emotional cues.

Therefore, as the anxiety bubbles up within them, they may not readily acknowledge what is going on. They feel the butterflies in their stomach, the tightening grip of fear that clinches their fists, and the rapid beating of one's heart in their ears that echoes impending doom and they do not know how to translate that and so they explode.

HOW TO DEAL WITH ANXIETY-RELATED BEHAVIOR ISSUES IN SCHOOL

- *Recognize the fear, even, and especially, if the child doesn't:* Verbally reassuring a child that he or she is experiencing worry is useful to the emotional student. Remember, many times children may not be aware that they are anxious. Their heart may be pounding, their palms sweaty, their brains clouded, and yet they cannot classify what is going on. If you have ever had a panic attack, you are likely to classify this unpleasantness as "a heart attack," when in reality it is simply a horrible wave of worry and anxiety.

Similarly, a child may not be able to put a finger on the nebulous emotion that is anxiety.

Yet, when you classify and normalize the emotion, they now have a means to verbalize what they are feeling—for example, stating, "You look like you are feeling worried; let's spend some time reading (or finding an activity that they can briefly turn to distract them)." To normalize a feeling, a child must first understand it.

- *Expect verbal pushback when you acknowledge fear or worry:* Admitting one's lack of perceived bravery is not easy. Moreover, in a group of peers who may be eager to tease, one's lack of confidence mercilessly is all the more difficult. Therefore, you may get "I am not worried/nervous/anxious/afraid" as a common pushback from a student. This sentiment is merely for the benefit of one's peers to "save face." Yet, if done discreetly, it shows that you are aware of what the student is feeling and can help him or her to identify his or her emotional experience as well. Therefore, quietly whispering your noticing of the student's anxiety and that this is okay will likely belie an empathetic response of relief.
- *Look for "what if" thinking:* Children, as well as adults, are always talking to themselves cognitively. It is the way we process the world around us, like a computer that has its hard drive constantly busy and loading the next string of data. The information is perceived as 100 percent our reality. Taken to an extreme, I once worked with an elderly man with posttraumatic stress disorder (PTSD) and paranoid schizophrenia. He believed he was in the midst of a battle in which he was fighting for the lives of his fellow soldiers and the innocent civilians around him. Telling him this did not exist would be like telling him his existence was a lie. It was real to him, and, therefore, it was real.

Children who are more anxious or worried tend to subscribe to "what if" thinking—that is, they unintentionally exaggerate with a negative brush what is *going* to happen and believe with 100 percent certainty that it is *going* to happen. This is generally amplified and/or triggered by a new experience, assignment, or social situation. This means that when you anticipate a new venture or deviation from the classroom routine or norm, you are best to explain in detail what to expect, what may be different, as well as what these particular pupils think could be "the worst-case scenario," following this up with what you would do to resolve such an unlikely occurrence of such an unlikely situation.

Why worst-case scenario? Because they have already believed that scenario will happen in their heads and they need someone to work this idea through to fruition and potential solution(s). In schools, we have drills for every imaginable situation so that we are prepared, do not panic, and know what to do. Anxious students need to be prepared and know what to do in the situations that constantly churn in their head with no resolution or answers.

- *Give two choices when choices are possible to be given:* Let's go back to the roller-coaster example or, better yet, the scenario of a fear of flying. What do these two potentially anxiety-provoking experiences have in common? They demonstrate an opportunity in which the passenger has little to no control over the situation. In a school setting (like mentioned in most of a child's life), control is almost in the sole domain of the educator. Without control or choices, anxiety can soar through the roof.

    Therefore, giving students choices, whenever possible, that you can live with are helpful in giving a child who is anxious some leverage in control as well as some grasp over worry. Choices, however, can also evoke worry, regarding "What if I make the wrong choice? Which choice is better? What if I make a decision and everyone laughs at me?" Hence, a limit (generally two or three) has to be provided to avoid children becoming overwhelmed with what to do when some control is placed in their laps.

- *Anxious students tend to shut down*: In the best-selling book *Emotional Intelligence*, Daniel Goleman, PhD, indicated that it takes twenty minutes to regain their emotional equilibrium after they have experienced a trigger of reactive emotions such as anger, anxiety, and fright.[1]

    So, how does that influence how you as an educator interact with a child who is experiencing a behavioral issue? Don't interact with the child, if possible, for at least twenty minutes.

    Think of it as a pot of boiling water. If you take a pot of boiling water off the stove, what happens? It rapidly ceases boiling. You put it back a few seconds later; what happens? Almost immediately a rolling boil, yet again.

    Take it off the stove, and let it settle to room temperature for a few minutes or so, and then place it back on the burner. It will take several minutes more to reach a boiling point again from the tepid point it went back to.

How is that a parallel to your work as an educator? If you continue to engage or upset students after an initial boil, previous to their system, returning to room temperature you have created a constant "reboiling." Inadvertently, or maybe even intentionally, you have not allowed their system to return to essentially "room temperature" or baseline functioning and triggered another behavioral issue (or even a wave of such behaviors).

THE ICEBERG OF ANGER

Let's take a relatively simplistic example that seems to be solely anger-inspired. A six-year-old goes with his parent to the supermarket. As the parent meanders through the aisles tossing groceries into the cart, they accidentally happen upon the toy aisle.

This raises the child's interest. The parent allows the child to look at the various assorted toys that litter the aisle. Then suddenly, the child finds it—the toy of a lifetime—for as long as a lifetime can seem for a child's minute-long attention span.

He asks, he begs, he pleads. But, alas, it is a "no go." He cannot budge his parent to spring for this toy that he has *always* wanted. He falls to the ground, kicks, and screams and even has some words that may make a trucker blush. Is this anger? On the surface, yes, absolutely!

However, if we look further, this seemingly simple interaction of this five-year-old shows he is experiencing a whole host of emotions. He is, of course, angry. Yet, he is also frustrated because his mother said "no." In addition, he is saddened because he had a whole *plan* of how that very toy was going to interact with his collection of toys back home; the plan is now dashed. In fact, he is actually grieving because there is a missing part of his imaginary world that is (at least temporarily) empty.

As an educator, be aware that whenever and wherever you see anger, know that this is just the tip of the proverbial iceberg. Swirling beneath this iceberg is the much larger foundation of other emotions that are at the core and need to be reached.

For instance, when you see an "angry" student, do you ask yourself or that student:

- Is he or she frustrated about something?
- Is he or she scared, anxious, or frustrated about something?
- Does he or she feel embarrassed or humiliated?
- Is he or she aware of these other emotions that are intertwined with what he or she believes he or she is feeling?

Asking these questions allows you to go "deeper than the anger." Find the origin of the behavior(s), and meet them where they are versus the superficial and overt behavior that you see—namely, the anger. Hence, when you see anger, ask about the other emotions that are associated.

DON'T TAKE YOURSELF SO SERIOUSLY

If you cannot joke and be lighthearted, you are more likely to be baited into negative attention-seeking behaviors by students. Why? Because they know that they can draw "the serious" teacher into a power struggle, far easier than someone who does not allow their emotions to be rattled because they wear their heart on their sleeves.

Humor helps avoid becoming easily burnt out and allows students to feel comfortable in your class. In addition, you save your proverbial "ammo," so to speak, for more major behavioral issues that you may need it for. If the students see that you "are serious" over the critical issues of maladaptive behaviors, they are more likely to take you seriously. This strategy is more compelling versus constant yelling, nagging, or screaming, which exponentially deteriorates your effectiveness.

DON'T EXPECT STUDENTS TO LEARN YOUR STYLE OF LEARNING

As mentioned earlier, students have a wide array of learning styles and needs. Pupils with behavioral and attention issues tend to learn in "small bite-size pieces" and through experiential and kinesthetic learning. If you have a different teaching style preference other than what your students embrace, it is important to tailor your style to their needs (not vice versa). Doing the opposite leads to an uphill struggle for learning. Ask yourself not "What am I teaching my students?"; rather ask yourself, "What are my students learning?" What we think we are teaching and what students are actually absorbing can be two very different concepts and can mean the difference between success and failure in a lesson.

THE "EITHER/OR" STATEMENT

If we are going to deliver a consequence to students, it should be logical and natural. What that means is it should be in an "either/or" context. "*Either* you do this *or* that happens." Such a statement allows a child to have a choice and recognizes potential consequences that will occur if they do not decide to do so. It is also how the so-called adult world works.

For instance:

- "*Either* you pay your mortgage *or* you lose your house."
- "*Either* you go the speed limit *or* you get a ticket."
- "*Either* you go grocery shopping *or* you are going to be hungry."

Remember that as an educator, discipline is also an educational opportunity. In other words, our thoughts should always be "How will this lesson (i.e., consequence) teach you something that will be valuable to you in the real world that you will inherit someday?" These are best known as logical and natural consequences. The idea is the "real world's laws" when you do something, naturally or logically, occur each and every time you do it. Put another way, the laws of the world will "break you," long before you "break them."

Life lessons are found within natural or logical consequences such as the following:

- *If* you break something, *you* have to pay for it or fix it.
- *If* you choose not to eat, *you* will be hungry.
- *If* you are mean to others, *they* may not be kind to you or trust you.
- *If* you do not work, *you* do not get the benefits found from completing your job.
- *If* you are late, *you* must make up the time somewhere else.
- *If* you do not prepare and practice, *you* are likely to not be as good or fail.
- *If* you don't try, *you* always fail.
- *If* you don't make mistakes, *you* will never learn to do it right.
- *If* you are upset, *you* must offer suggestions for a solution.

How do these consequences translate to discipline in the public education forum?

- *If* a child writes on his desk, *he or she* has to clean it up during recess.
- *If* a child chooses not to eat his or her lunch in a timely manner in the cafeteria, *he or she* will be hungry the remainder of the day.
- *If* you are not kind to others during class, *they* will not play with you at recess until you learn better ways to engage them.
- *If* you waste fifteen minutes fooling around in class, *you* will have to spend fifteen minutes at recess, after school, or at home doing that work, when you would rather be doing another activity.
- *If* you are late for school, *you* will have to make up that much time at some other time, inconvenient to your own schedule.
- *If* you cannot schedule time to study or practice, *then* this will have to be "built" into your day (much like soccer or dance practice).
- *If* you do not try, does this make *you* feel better or worse about yourself?
- *If* you are "sulking" or angry, *you* must talk out potential solutions, as we cannot read your mind.

APPLICATION OF LITTLE LIFE LESSONS: LOGICAL AND NATURAL CONSEQUENCES

Remember, natural and logical consequences are akin to "laws of life"—that is, the wisdom or rules and potential consequences that almost always naturally evolve from not following them. It is not necessary to harp or belabor your point with these consequences. You are late, you make it up, you do not come to school on time, and the time comes out of your leisure that is somewhere inconvenient to you.

- A student hurts another student's feelings; he writes a note of apology on his time (i.e., recess, home).
- The student spends fifteen minutes gabbing with her peer; she has to spend time at recess or after school.
- A student engages in negative behavior; he must accept responsibility by explaining it to his parents via the telephone.
- The student lies; he must confront/face those he lied to, despite the discomfort in doing so.
- A student refuses to do homework/tells a parent that he is doing homework the correct way; he has to face the teacher the next day.
- The student cuts the line; he goes to the back of the line.
- The student does not fulfill responsibilities in an extracurricular activity; he is temporarily halted from engaging in that activity.
- The student refuses to eat what is for lunch; he is hungry the rest of the day.
- The pupil "tears up" the room; the pupil has to put everything back.

Remember, these rules have a natural negative consequence. Students must learn that the choices are theirs to make, but the consequences that arise are theirs to have to accept as well. It is perhaps the first and hardest lesson of the "real world" that we are preparing them for. Or as Robert Kiyosaki quoted, "In the real world, the smartest people are people who make mistakes and learn. In school, the smartest people don't make mistakes."[2]

NOTES

1. Daniel Goleman, *Emotional Intelligence* (New York: Bantam Books, 2006).

2. Asad Meah. "35 Inspirational Quotes On Mistakes." Awaken the Greatness Within, Asad Meah, 25 Feb. 2018, awakenthegreatnesswithin.com/35-inspirational-quotes-on-mistake/.

Chapter 5

The Student

It All Boils Down to the Customer

If kids come to us from strong, healthy functioning families, it makes our job easier. If they do not come to us from strong, healthy, functioning families, it makes our job more important.

—Barbara Coloroso

"Where is Ms. Smith's class?" Alyssa is a new thirteen-year-old student in what seems to be in an impossibly large middle school. She checks her crumpled-up map of the school and becomes increasingly anxious as she paces ever faster down the infinite hallways toward an uncertain destination.

She is concerned about who will be friends with her. What will her teachers be like? Will she know the new curriculum of yet another school? All these ideas flash in her head.

Anger, anxiety, frustration, and fear swirl all around her. She tries to swallow hard and swat them away like flies. Yet, they come back.

What is she going to do?

So, if we are going to be successful in our quest with students, we must know what they know in order to achieve what we want to achieve.

STUDENTS HAVE TRICKS OF THE TRADE TOO, YOU KNOW!

So, you have spent your time in expensive professional development workshops and years in college and are now reading this book regarding the ever-popular subjects of classroom and behavior management. Thus, the hope is to sharpen your knowledge of techniques and build your cache of skills for your chosen profession.

But have you thought that your students also have learned strategies to get what they want? Children constantly observe just about from the moment of their birth. They learn from what adults and others around them do versus what they say. Quickly, all too quickly, they grasp what works and what does not work in their behalf. They too develop skills and tools and put them into quick effect to get what they need or want.

STUDENTS DO WHAT WORKS

From the beginning of their time on this earth, children are learning what works and what does not work. Therefore, when you see a behavior, ask yourself: Why are they doing it? Most behaviors have a specific purpose or reason.

IS IT TRULY OUT OF CONTROL?

Often, in the halls of our schools, we hear the words, "That kid is outta control!" Now, the question becomes, is that *really true*? Out of control means, by simple definition, that a child cannot control (or help) what he or she is doing.

If a behavior is *truly* "out of control," that should mean that you will see that behavior generally "pops up" in most (if not all) environments where and when the student is present. We should see the similar "out of control" behavior at school, at home, on the bus, in karate class, and at other places because a child cannot keep such a behavior under wraps for any period of time.

If we see a behavior in a single place, we must question, is the behavior truly defined as *out* of control? Or is the behavior *somewhat* controlled based upon the environment that the student is involved in?

If the behavior is only in a single or a few limited environments, this is indicative of an opportunity to make headway regarding that behavior.

THE TYPES OF STUDENTS YOU WILL ENCOUNTER AS YOU GO

In your career, you will meet many, perhaps thousands of, students along the way. After several years, you will begin to notice a pattern of children who have similar or identical behaviors. Though you will see many different names and faces, you will observe parallels of how children interact and react in a classroom setting. It is then you can apply interventions more globally to the other students who you will encounter along the road of your career and who are similar to those previous students.

"THE PARROT"

When a child is a typically developing infant, he or she will see an obstacle and he or she will try to get around it, over it, and under it or push it, if he or she wants to get at what is on the other side. We call this persistence of a normal developmental milestone of growth.

Children have enormous willpower when they want something, and so, sometimes, they will attempt to continue to "peck away" at a parent or educator to get what they want on the other side. The students question, repeat, or try to get their way with the teacher/authority figure until they are assured it will not work.

At home, such a strategy may work relatively frequently. The parents become so tired of the constant pestering that they throw up their hands and say, "Just do it already; just leave me the heck alone!" So, they try a similar strategy with a parallel adult (namely, the teacher). If it works on the second, third, or tenth try, then they will do it again and again and again. They learn to work harder, even if it is not generally smarter, with the idea that they must tear down an adult's resistance.

WITH "THE PARROT" CONSIDER THE FOLLOWING

- *Don't get pulled into the "power struggle" trap:* When you confront these pupils directly, you engage in a power struggle. Avoid engaging these students when possible, until they end their constant badgering.
- *Use a mantra:* If you do need to engage these students, do not raise your voice, show emotion, or change the context of your dialogue. Repeat the same statement repeatedly (like a mantra) of what it is specifically that you want them to do. "I need you to sit down before we can talk; I need you to sit down before we can talk." Doing so helps avoid them pulling you in and/ or you giving in to them.
- *Don't threaten or give in:* If you offer empty threats versus realistic consequences, the students will learn that they can win this struggle and not respect your authority. If this is truly an important situation to "dig your feet in," you will find that you are teaching children to simply work harder to get what they want, if you simply *give in*. Giving in is equated with winning the battle in "The Parrot's" strategy.

THE "I DON'T CARE" PUPIL

Think back to when you were a spry, young seventeen-year-old. You had the world at your fingertips, with a fresh-faced license and keys to go literally anywhere. Then, your parent tells you, "You are grounded!" Due to one of numerous parental indiscretions you allegedly violated, you are told, "No car for you tonight!"

Suddenly, your enthusiasm is deflated quicker than the air in a slashed set of tires. The date, the movies, the night out with your friends—all gone. GONE! You are angry. You are devastated. In your short, seventeen years of life, this is the worst thing that has ever happened to you! Ever!

So, how do you respond to this parental slight? With a tirade of anger and profanity, a debate listing all the reasons why you need the car, or maybe a vital plea for a parental pardon for this consequence? Most teens choose a far different strategy, that of feigning a lack of concern and caring. The simple response is the rallying cry of "I don't care."

It makes no sense, as it is a counterintuitive response. The teens care, and yet, they attempt to portray the very opposite. Why? Because if youth were to show their proverbial "hand of cards," they put themselves at a distinct disadvantage. Now, with this information, the parent knows where "to hit them where it hurts." So, the youth put on a poker face of "I don't care." This "I don't care" statement is a means of protecting themselves from punishment intertwined with pride.

Doing so avoids the problem of parents using meaningful consequences. It makes discipline as slippery as holding a lathered bar of soap. Younger children, similarly, adopt the same strategy with adults (educators and parents alike). "Don't care" equates to "I won't let you know what bothers me." So, this means when a consequence is effective, expect to hear, initially, "I don't care." Use that as a catalyst for guiding your consequences.

WITH THE "I DON'T CARE" PUPIL

- *Don't be fooled by the "I don't care" statement:* A student who states that he or she does not care is hoping that you will back off of whatever it is that you are trying to enforce. This means that you must use these consequences specifically in your toolbox of discipline.
- *Make them aware of their emotion:* Some "I don't care" students do not realize that the emotion that they generate greatly contrasts from what they are showing. For instance, when a child says, "I don't care," but is red in the face, yelling and stomping, it is helpful to let that child know that his or her feeling does not belie what is truly going on. Why is this so vital? Because an apathetic student (or one who claims he or she "doesn't care") may have convinced himself or herself he or she cannot change. Yet, the emotion the student is showing is precisely the energy he or she needs to change.

- *Learn what they "do care" about:* As mentioned earlier, prior to a conflict with these students, it is very useful to know what these pupils do care about. This can be done through a reinforcement inventory. That is what they truly care about, in the unlikely event that you may actually be addressing an issue that is not impactful to them.

THE "CLOSE OUT"

Ever go on social media and see on someone's "wall" and see a vague statement like, "Worst day of my life . . . I hate everything!"? Now, everyone concerned about the person's cryptic posting asks, "What is the matter? What happened? Are you okay? What can I do?" The person who posted this concerning tweet? Crickets. No response. Others are left to guess, talk about the person in worried tones toward others, and bear the concerns and sympathies about the person's potential plight.

How does a child use this? When a child "shuts down," this is generally defined by putting his or her head down and evading eye contact or to engage the teacher or other individuals. Often this is combined with the crossing of the arms as well as the obligatory pulling up of the hood.

As educators, we abhor a vacuum. We usually fill silence in classes with lecture, and we answer questions or encourage continuous dialogue. So when a student puts his or her head down or refuses engagement, it is our natural inclination to question, "What is the matter? What do you need? Do your work!" The issue then becomes that such actions play directly into that behavior. We are feeding and supporting the behavior by giving the closed-down pupil all the attention in the class. He or she has usurped the focus of the teacher and the class to the peril of those children who are doing what they should do and not vying for any more attention than any of their peers.

IF YOU HAVE A "CLOSE OUT" IN YOUR CLASS

- *Determine first if it is actually anxiety:* There is a huge difference between anxiety-based "shutting down" and "shutting down" as a means of manipulation. If the child is anxious, we must verbally address this. If it is manipulative in nature, we must not.
- *"Close out time" equals wasted time:* If a child wastes time while using a "close out" technique, this should be equated with wasted time. When you waste time and "close out" the world of your own responsibilities, you owe something. That something is that amount of time owed in the form of meeting those obligations at some other juncture in time, which may very

well be inconvenient to you. Hence, "close out time" should be measured, and that time will be owed at some other hour that is not expedient to the child (i.e., lunch, recess, after school, home). It is a lesson learned time that will not be "wasted"; it will just be "owed."

THE "FINE WHINE"

If you are a fan of great wines, you may try to visit Tuscany or maybe the smaller vineyards that dot our country. There are many fine wines: White, Red, Chablis, Rose, and the child. What is that? You don't like the whine of the child?

It is as bitter and caustic as vinegar of a formally sweet wine when allowed to spoil. This "whine" is annoying and often results in great gnashing of teeth among parents and educators alike. Often, it works because adults simply cannot bear to hear the scratching of the chalkboard sounds.

If you have a "fine whine" student in your class, the following may be useful to decrease the prevalence of whining in your classroom:

- *Don't answer the request:* When you respond to whining, you are subtly accepting that you are willing to engage in dialogue with the students.
- *Ask them to rephrase the statement:* Telling them to rephrase the statement in a less caustic tone will help in reinforcing what you want them to do.
- *Reward them immediately with your attention:* When children are not whining, only then you can reinforce them with your attention.

THE "GUILT MAGNET"

We all want to be the best educators and/or parents we can be. In fact, generally, any negative criticism toward this end seems to stick to us like a magnet. Not certain of this? Think of the most positive statement ever made to you by your parent? Now, recall the most negative and hurtful comment? Which is easier to recall? If you are like most people, generally, you can remember the most hurtful remarks. We are hardwired to soak those in and take them to heart.

Now, imagine you are a parent (if you are not already). The vocation of parenthood, much like an educator, is a very human and personal relationship. You are in charge of sculpting the future of an impressionable, young mind. So when a child says, "You hate me, you don't love me, you are the worst parent ever!" the guilt cuts to the heart of a parent's very being. The parent, in turn, will convince the child (and himself or herself) otherwise.

After learning and perfecting this skill at home, a child comes to school with the belief that guilt works and is an effective tool to bend adults to my whim. The problem is, in addition to it being ineffective and manipulative, it creates a far more insidious issue for the child. Initially, this is a tool kids may use to get their way. However, as time progresses and they constantly use this strategy, they start to actually believe the negative comments, and thus, it no longer becomes solely a defense mechanism but a cognitive belief and defensive mechanism. Now, it becomes "Everyone hates me, I can't do it, etc.," with no longer the goal of distracting an adult so they can get what they want. Rather, now it is how they cope with barriers of life and they tear down their self-image and self-esteem accordingly.

TO AVOID GETTING DRAWN INTO THE "GUILT MAGNET"

- *Don't get "pulled in":* When children say, "You hate me," or the alternative, "I hate you," we sometimes try to convince them otherwise. Do not do so, as this is just validating their empty words by getting down on their level.
- *Have them debate the false facts:* The most critical downside of the guilt magnet's strategy is to eventually become self-destructive. Hence, when they state that "no one likes me or you hate me, etc.," make them give three reasons to the contrary (i.e., "Tell me three people who like you or three things you like about yourself"). Doing so serves for the youth to debate distorted thinking that serves to decrease their self-image and personal worth.

THE "PERFECTIONIST"

Sometimes, we think that students are avoiding a task because they stubbornly just don't want to do it. In reality, they hold themselves to such a high bar that they do not believe they can do it "perfectly." So why bother at all? They further frustrate themselves because they notice what they believe to be their glaring imperfections and choose to do nothing versus be reminded that they cannot do the skills as well as they wished.

WITH THE "PERFECTIONIST"

- *With these students it is critical that we seek a "good enough":* We ask them to make mistakes and recognize "what is the worst thing that can happen."
- *Break academics into smaller, manageable pieces:* These students quickly become overwhelmed when they look at an assignment as a whole. Encourage them to separate schoolwork/activities into smaller "chunks."

- *Avoid comparison with others:* In case of some children who stay in a constant state of rivalry with others, remind them it is not a competition against others but just to be the best me that they can be.
- *Help them to see that "what if" scenario:* These students always see the worst-case scenario. Help them to take a step back and realize, "What is the worst thing that can happen?" Encourage them to think the absolute worst case and then help them to debate that they can handle it with the support of others.
- *Avoid "black and white" thinking:* These children will often use words that indicate a dramatic level of inflexible thinking in their thought process. They use works like "never, always, should." Have them question this thinking, and look for the gray areas that they fail to see in between.

"THE CLOWN"

As we have discussed previously, the surest way to garner the maximum amount of attention in the quickest means possible is via negative behavior. The best way to attempt to gain control is by being the class clown and heckling the teacher or your peers to get a snicker or a giggle. The "class clown" enjoys making others laugh and gaining the spotlight for his or her stand-up routine.

WHEN YOU RUN INTO "THE CLOWN," REMEMBER

- *A clown's tool is always humor:* If you can utilize a sense of appropriate lightheartedness, you take the wind out of their sails. Also, not feeding attention into "the clown's" antics helps to avoid them gaining control of the class.
- *Don't create a studio audience:* If you are going to speak with them, do it on a one-on-one basis. This avoids them using the conversation to be transformed into additional funny back-and-forth banter, which embarrasses the teacher and serves for the educator to lose his or her authority.
- *Clowns sometimes step over the line:* Sometimes "the clown" simply does not always realize boundaries and crossing the line. If you can provide a means of letting them know that they are crossing the boundaries of appropriate behavior in a subtle, agreed-upon way (e.g., a tug on your ear), which is agreed upon by both of you ahead of time, this can avoid this issue.
- *Clowns believe that ALL laughter pays off:* Clowns don't always realize the balance between funny and insulting. They believe that if they get the majority of peers' laughter, that is the payoff. They sometimes don't realize that humor can simultaneously be funny to some while hurtful to others.

Making them aware of this seemingly obvious fact is critical. In addition, letting them know that if a comment is funny to some and not others, it is *generally not funny* in the realm of social skills.

* *Finally, take the audience away from the clown or the clown away from the audience:* Every comedian loves an audience. If you have a clown, take him or her away from the audience or vice versa, with as little disruption as possible.

"THE SULKER"

This is the students who cross their arms, look down, and refuse to engage the teacher because of some perceived slight or they're not getting their way. They look like "the close out," except they try harder to know that they are upset and want your attention. "The sulker" likes to suck you into their vacuum. Meaning in their semi-silence (aside from the grunts and stomps), we try to fill the void with our own words or statements. No matter what you say, they answer, "No!" They continue to refuse your suggestions or interventions. They like to stonewall but still be "loud enough" in their silence to get your attention.

What to Do with a "Sulker":

* *Don't try to climb the stone wall:* "Sulkers" are used to adults giving them undue attention for their negative and ineffective behaviors. As they get older, they will learn the hard way that when you sulk or create drama, your peers and the world work around you and not with you.
* *Don't let them off the hook:* "Sulkers" are used to being let off the hook when they are done sulking. They believe that all is forgiven and they should move on from the free pass they assume that occurred from their designated "sulking" time. They must learn that they are still responsible for the time they wasted. They may give pushback for this; however, when you feel sorry for yourself at work, does that give you a free pass from your job responsibilities? Hence, you are providing them a junior version of a very adult lesson.

"THE BULLY"

A whole book can be written on the subject of bullying. Throughout your life, you will find bullies who take what they want or hurt others without regard. Nevertheless, we still have to tackle this subject because it is a necessary and critical topic in the realm of students you will face.

First, it is important to remember where bullies lurk. It is often out of the gaze of teachers. Therefore, we must do everything we can to negate the peer influence and acceptance of this behavior. In addition, specific lessons conducted within the classroom on antibullying and conflict resolution skills are useful (though not the be-all and end-all). Finally, addressing these issues immediately is necessary as they don't tend to get any better without immediate and concrete action.

Specific policies that outline what bullying is, and just as importantly, what it is not should be shared with students, parents, and all educators. In addition, students, parents, and teachers must know the protocol for reporting this behavior and recognize that it is not "ratting another out." If need be, provide them a "bully box" where the issue can be addressed anonymously.

There are a number of reasons why children bully; however, we can help to address these proactively in a number of ways:

1. *Bullies can have difficulty with empathy:* Teaching a child to understand others before seeking to be understood is a skill that takes time to address. However, a community of empathetic students provides less of a chance of letting bullying grow and fester. In 2014, the *Huffington Post* conducted a survey in thirty-five schools across the nation with over 10,000 children to measure the level of empathy they perceived in their respective schools. In the educational settings where students said they had greater levels of empathy, children also noted a much lower incidence of bullying.[1]
2. *Low frustration and anger threshold:* Assisting in developing skills for self-soothing and anger management skills, school-wide, as well as teaching assertiveness techniques. Children who don't know how to assert themselves gravitate to either passivity or aggression.
3. *A belief that they have no control or power:* Children typically have little control or power within their own lives. Giving them power, when possible, to make appropriate choices puts the perception of power back in their hands. In addition, speaking with families to see other potential areas of perceived powerlessness is also a valuable strategy.
4. *Coach children where it is needed:* Bullying, as we mentioned before, takes place generally on the bus, at lunchroom, or during recess. These are the places that school counselors can act as "life coaches" to teach alternative ways of handling conflict in the practical and real-life settings when adult guidance is usually least available.

"THE TANTRUMER": IT IS ALL DOWNHILL FROM THERE

Have you ever tried to stop a roller coaster going downhill? Certainly it would be difficult, if not impossible, to stop a vehicle going at that speed, immediately. In fact, using a time-tested scientific theory, Newton's first law of motion is often stated as "an object at rest stays at rest and an object in motion stays in motion with the same speed and in the same direction unless acted upon by an unbalanced force."[2]

Once a youth has gone over the proverbial "edge," it may simply be too late. The tantrum may have to play itself out to some degree. That being said, it is key to keep the other pupils, the student and those around, safe during this situation.

In doing so, it is vital that you eliminate a potential audience as they can serve to fuel the behavior and are generally the bystanders most in danger of getting hurt. Therefore, isolating the student with few competent faculty who do not serve to irritate the student is key. Keep in mind that you may actually be the one who agitates the student; perhaps it is best to have others involved and let your ego stand out of the way.

Listen to the student's complaints. Often tantruming is correlated with verbalization as to what the complaint is, such as, "It is not fair!" "He/she was starting with me!" "Everyone is always on her/his side!" Whatever the issue that is being voiced, it is best to not try to rationalize that the student is wrong. Remember that emotions are not logical and vice versa. Listen versus trying to convince the students that they are wrong about the origin of their anger or are not entitled to their respective emotions.

For instance, when a child calls a teacher or peer "an a**hole," it is obvious this is hostile and aggressive communication. What is not clear under this seemingly vague label is what "a**hole" means. Now, it is recognized what part of the anatomy it refers to. Rather, it refers to that this global statement simply does not have much helpful detail to the recipient or the student.

So, when a student utilizes four letters of profanity in his or her vocabulary, we have to help clarify this from an aggressive paradigm to that of a productive dialogue that can be useful in nature. This means, "You sound like you are mad at Joe; help me to understand what he did." Clarifying and targeting the issue helps to specify and pinpoint how to handle it.

WHAT DO WE DO WITH "THE TANTRUMER?"

- *Look for the underlying emotion:* As we discussed earlier, the emotion that is most apparent in a tantrum is that of anger. It is easy for those intervening to be drawn into and feed that reactive emotion. However, don't get drawn into this. Seek to find the deeper emotions that are triggering the behavior. Bring to light the sadness, frustration, or fears that are the core emotions leading to the tantrum.
- *Don't feed the fire:* Did you ever notice we feed the things we want least? We feed a tantrum with all sorts of attention. We feed it with anger, talking,

and emotional attention. Thus, we get more of what we don't want and less of what we do want. Feed the positive, and starve the negative tantrum.

- *Remember twenty minutes before back in the pool:* As a child you may have remembered that you were told that you could not go back into the pool for twenty to thirty minutes after you ate. The fear was a devastating cramp would cause you to double over in pain midstroke and causing you to drop like a rock. Well, as it turns out, this may have been an old wives' tale; however, twenty minutes have another good rule of thumb. As we mentioned earlier, Dr. Daniel Goleman, of *Emotional Intelligence* fame, indicated it takes twenty minutes after a tantrum ceases before a child's emotional volatility returns to normal levels.[3]

THE PROFANITY PURVEYOR

Often, along with anger and tantruming come cursing and profane language. This verbal diarrhea of unkind words could leave a trucker blushing and a teacher questioning whether they are educating or exorcising the children.

Don't get drawn into this. However, keep in mind that children who are engaging in behavioral issues often label those around them in stark "black-and-white" terms. This means that everyone is for or against them (but mostly against them). Often, this paranoia is communicated via cursing. It is far easier to place labels via cursing and then say hurtful barbs at those who show caring toward you.

Concurrently, it becomes far too easy for adults to get snagged into the "lack of respect" trap when they hear these four-letter expletives being weaved together by these talented young virtuosos. However, this perspective is superficial in nature and fails to look into the true origin of the problem.

Primarily, to gain respect, one must show a student by modeling continuous good behavior. Avoid getting thrown off that pedestal by a power struggle trap of empty and profane personality attacks.

Also, look at the cursing dialogue as something of a poor communication skill versus a full frontal attack.

As an example, let's look at the following scenario:

Student: "You are an a**hole!"

Educator: "You seem very upset and angry. Help me understand what you are upset about."

Student: "I am not upset! You are just an a**hole!"

Educator: "I notice that you are raising your voice and you look angry. I am confused. What do you need to help you?"

Student: "I need everyone to leave me the f***ing alone!"

Educator: "So, you need some time for others to not bother you. Can we figure out a place for you to just hang out and chill?"

The issue with this type of communication is that it is clearly aggressive. However, it is also, just as clearly, unproductive. Why? Because the four-letter verbiage that the student is using like a fine artist of four-letter words does not say anything useful in solving the problem.

Why are they an "a**hole"? What do you need to make this issue better? What did they do wrong? What do you need from others to best support you?

We often get caught up in the words and do not recognize the message in the anger. Hence, we look at *what* they are saying versus *how* they are saying it. We negate that the child is unable to communicate needs, much as that of any of other student with a communication issue.

Many will say, "Well, when they get in the real world, if they curse at their boss or at others in society, they will be punched, fired, or arrested." Very true, however, it is our goal to harshly expose them to the "real world" or, alternatively, to help them learn navigation skills as that world comes ever closer to their grasp.

Do you let them get away with cursing and disrespecting? No, but the time to address a tirade of cursing is not the optimal time when they have the least amount of skills at their disposal (in the middle of a behavior). It is after when they are settled down and are able to fully absorb and understand their behavior and potential consequences (not in the proverbial thick of the battle).

"THE REVERSE PARROT TECHNIQUE"

Remember the tool when students attempt to "peck away" at the adult's patience by repeatedly voicing their wants? It turns out that this turning the tables is sometimes an effective means of getting a student to do what you want as well.

For instance, continuing to state what you want the students to do with the exact same words and emotional tone (like a monotonous mantra) creates a "verbal wall" in which they cannot get over, around, or through, by arguing, emotional reaction, or distraction. In doing so, they rapidly recognize that it is far easier to comply than to continue to fight a losing, uphill battle.

For example:

Student: "I am not listening to you. I want to go to recess and that's it!"

Educator: "When you sit down in your seat quietly, we will discuss how much of recess you will miss." (Calm voice tone)

Student: "I don't care what you say! I am going to go outside!"

Educator: "When you sit down in your seat quietly, we will discuss how much of recess you will miss." (Calm voice tone)

Student: "I am going outside! No matter what you say. . . I don't care!"

Educator: "When you sit down in your seat quietly, we will discuss how much of recess you will miss." (Calm voice tone, same dialogue).

Student: "Fine! I'll sit down (sits down in a huff)! Can we talk now?"

Now, the dialogue can shift to expectations of students' behavior and what their options are.

"THE STUCK GEAR SHIFT" STUDENT

Children with behavioral issues are notoriously bad at "shifting gears." When we discuss this issue, we will look at it from two paradigms, both of which influence a student's behavior in different ways.

The first occurs when we ask them to go to physical education class, thus running around and getting sweaty. Then, only a few minutes later, we ask them to immediately shift into the cognitive rigors of academic work again. For many children they can take this dynamic change in expectations, handle it, and move on.

For those with behavioral issues, however, they tend to have difficulty in recognizing and adjusting to a new series of expectations at the "drop of a dime." This means, while the rest of the students are back doing math work, the pupil with potential behavioral issues is still trying to calm down a racing mind and body that is still geared to running around and the physical requirements of a physical education (PE) class paradigm. Or, to put it another way, it is like moving from a hot tub to an ice bath in one foul swoop and not expecting to freeze or go into shock.

FOR "THE STUCK GEAR SHIFT STUDENT"

• *The first aspect is preparation:* If you were driving down the darkened highway with no headlights, your anxiety of the open road ahead would likely be through the roof. Similarly, when a child does not know what to expect next (or does not adequately prepare for it), the behavioral consequences can be disastrous.

  Therefore, as you are moving into the next event of a day, tell these pupils what is expected of them in some degree of detail.

• *Do not force a radical gear shift:* Avoid having physical and heavily academic activities back to back. For example, recess and math, PE and reading. Doing so taxes a student's brain and body to create an academic "whiplash" of sorts.

• *Use a pictorial and written schedule of the day:* Be certain both are clearly visible, and help the children to discern where they feel in control of what is coming down the road of life, scholastically. Remember, when you are angry and have steam coming out of your ears, you are less likely to read, hear, and comprehend. You are still likely to be able to visualize a schedule, however.

The next challenge with the "stuck gear shift" is in the behavior itself. When children become engaged in a behavior, they develop a downward cycle in which all that they can focus on is the behavior or the presenting problem itself.

In other words, if they feel wronged or frustrated, they just cannot leave that issue alone. They keep obsessing, and their mood keeps swirling downward around the issue itself. The child is emotionally "stuck" and quite simply cannot move on.

MORE INTERVENTIONS FOR THE "EMOTIONALLY STUCK" STUDENT

• *Use of "emotional dynamite":* When a student is stuck intractably in the muck of negative emotion, it may become necessary to force the gear shift into another aspect. For instance, having a toolbox of items that a student can turn to when angry can be useful. In it contain items that are simple and tactile in nature: fuzzy balls; soft clay; and items that can be stretched, are tactile, cannot be broken, and cannot cause injury. Often times, Occupational Therapists (OPs) or Physical Therapists (PTs) have a bevy of such items that other educators can borrow.

THE BEN FRANKLIN EFFECT OF EMOTIONAL DYNAMITE TECHNIQUE

This time-tested technique is named after the famous politician, scientist, and Renaissance man Ben Franklin. The Ben Franklin Effect is a common psychological phenomenon that details how people wind up liking you *more* when they do you a favor.[4]

So how can this be translated to an effective intervention in the school setting? Quite simply, have something simple, attention-provoking, and helpful (or seemingly so) that can take advantage of this basic human tendency.

Clarifying the Technique of the Ben Franklin Effect in the School Setting

Let's look at a potential educational example of this effect. Have a plastic jar with coins that can be "accidentally dropped" on the floor. Immediately, requesting the student to assist the educator in putting the coins in the jar served two vital purposes: (1) it takes advantage of the Ben Franklin Effect to harness the pupil's desire to gain control and assist the teacher/educator and (2) the loud sound and physical activity "snap" the child out of listening to those deafening emotional gears of anger. Finally, after "helping" the teacher/educator, they can now move on to the next activity rapidly without any time for the youth to think of what occurred previously.

PINPOINTING A STUDENT'S WEAKNESSES

Think about the teaching style(s) many of us in education employ. Most of it is the teacher speaking and the students diligently listening. They take notes, raise their hands at determined junctures, and answer questions in a respectful fashion. Now, we all (theoretically) recognize that students have varying forms of learning—from visual to auditory to kinesthetic and so on—and so we have (or should have) over the past many years adapted teaching accordingly.

Nevertheless, the vast majority of education is still done in an auditory format. Further, most educators are comfortable in solely using this format, as it is the simplest means of getting information from teacher to pupil. According to Ricki Linksman, MEd, many youths seen at National Reading Diagnostics Institute in Illinois have been given a formal diagnosis of attention-deficit/hyperactivity disorder (ADHD). Looking further, reading evaluations of these youngsters often display that, rather than having an attention disorder, they are most accurately kinesthetic learners. Of even greater interest, Linksman notes, when provided the opportunity to learn through a kinesthetic framework, their ADHD-like behavior often disappears.[5]

You may say, wait a minute, the children we deal with have behavioral issues, not ADHD. Interestingly, however, a Danish study by psychiatrists Jensen and Steinhausen of 14,825 children and adolescents (aged four to seventeen years) determined that 52 percent of the study population had at least one other emotional disorder (aside from ADHD), and 26.2 percent had two or more additional mental disorders.[6]

Therefore, the more engaged students you have, the better. In our current world of technology, children seek an interactive experience. In fact, many argue their brains are rewired for such immersive experiences.

To engage students kinesthetically:

- Avoid extended periods of auditory and lecturing.
- Use a great deal of movement in your classroom (yourself and students).
- Display a great deal of energy and humor (and allow for the same).
- Break down long tasks to smaller "chunks" that they can digest and allow for some time to expend energy in between.
- Provide "hands-on" tools for learning.
- If they prefer to stand up or "fidget" while doing work, remember, the goal is the ultimate product.

THESE STUDENTS ARE SENSITIVE AND LACK SENSITIVITY

Children with behavioral issues can be a lesson in contrasts. For example, they may lack awareness of their surroundings, yet they are very sensitive of the stimuli that are around them. As an example, a child with an acting-out behavior, because he or she is uncomfortable, can be attributed to being in a humid, sweltering classroom. Yet, the child cannot pinpoint to you that this is the source of discontent. He or she will scream and tantrum versus being able to verbalize the concerns or needs fully.

Sometimes it may feel like working with a toddler, in which you are pointing aimlessly, trying to figure out the needs or wants when they are acting out and you cannot figure out why.

The following, however, are things to think about when you have a student with potential behavioral issues:

- Are they too hot or too cold?
- Are they hungry?
- Are they sick?
- Are they tired?
- Are they uncomfortable about what they are wearing, sitting, or doing?
- Are they confused or anxious?

THE CHILDREN ARE RESILIENT THEORY

We often hear that children are resilient. They are able to go through the most difficult of circumstances and come out on the other end relatively unscathed. The question is, is that actually true?

First, if you think about any major trauma you may have experienced in your life, you had not much of a choice but to do what you needed to do. It was not that you were moving on, but rather it was that you were existing through the crisis. Often, later down the line, it "catches up with you." Like a train barreling down the tracks, you can only use your limits of psychological defenses for so long, before they falter and you are left to handle the issue at hand. Hence, we don't usually talk of "current trauma"; rather, we call it "posttrauma."

Similarly, children who have experienced traumatic issues must move on. They are not given a choice because the wave of life itself sweeps them forward. Yet, as the trauma explodes around them, they are thrown backward by that same blast. We should be on the lookout for what are regressive behaviors due to kids being traumatized versus behavioral issues that seem merely attention-seeking.

This means that as an educator, it is important to know the recent history of what went on (or, if possible, changes at home) for a student, prior to them coming to you. It may seem like common sense, however, in the ever-growing job responsibilities of an educator; it is vital to know how history and posttrauma can affect behaviors.

Children with posttraumatic issues must be especially reassured that they are safe in school, routine is going to be preserved, and those who surround them are going to address them in a calm and steady manner. In addition, integrating relaxation skills into the school day curriculum can benefit all students (especially those with behaviors or trauma issues).

BASIC GUIDED IMAGERY

1. Find a quiet, regular time during the school day that the class is least likely to be disturbed.
2. Have class close their eyes and imagine their favorite place or vacation for relaxation.
3. Have each student imagine what they would see, smell, hear, and feel in this favored place. Have pupils concentrate on each and every detail of these sights, sounds, and senses, until you can look around and imagine being in this place yourself.
4. Take deep, relaxing breaths as you go from where you are to the imaginary place that you want to be.
5. Slowly open your eyes, and ease yourself back into your daily classroom routine.

THE WEAKNESS OF NOT RECOGNIZING STRENGTHS

As we have discussed earlier, most children are generally egocentric—that is, they only see what is directly in front of them and everything that happens in the world revolves around something they did or did not do. In short, they are the sun and the universe orbits around their small place in this world.

Children with behaviors are no different; however, their behaviors tend to garner more negative reactions among those around them. Youth with behavioral issues fail to recognize that they make poor choices until it is far too late. They then have difficulty recognizing the cause, what they did as their response, and the consequences of their actions. However, because they are also egocentric, they come to believe that they are inherently "bad." That is very different than making a poor choice or decision. They believe "bad decisions" are who/what they believe they are. Sometimes, this is further reinforced by parents who (unintentionally) point out behaviors as who they are versus the choices they make.

For example:

Educator: "You have a choice to go to math, or you will have to make up that work after school. I know you are able to make good choices."

Educator: "Either you can do your work now or you will have to bring it home and do it instead of playing your video games. I really hope you make a good choice so that you can play that new game you have."

START OFF THE DAY WITH STRENGTHS

Many of our students with behavioral issues have low self-worth and value. This can be due to mental health issues, difficult home life, developmental disabilities, and so forth. With more and more focus on curriculum and standardized testing, it becomes easy for a student's mental well-being to get thrown out with the bathwater of sheer academics and requirements.

Starting out the day with sincere compliments and recognition of class-wide strengths is a good routine to begin in school/class. Keep in mind that it must be done for the whole class. You can provide students compliments or you can do the following:

1. Have students give themselves one compliment or strength each day that they see in themselves.
2. Have each student give a single compliment to a peer (appropriate in nature) that they don't usually associate with until everyone has had a chance.
3. The teacher gives one behavioral, specific compliment to each student on a daily or weekly basis.

That pesky question likely arises yet again, "How will I have time for that, with time for this, with the host of other things that I have to do daily?" Do it when you can, but do it regularly and on a schedule. The children who have behavioral issues need that. The positive thoughts may be the only such sentiments they hear (including from themselves). As Frederick Douglass quotes, "It is easier to build strong children than to repair broken men (or women)."

"THE CRAP SANDWICH"

In counseling people there is an informal "1:5 rule." This rule recognizes that human nature tends to have negative statements stick to us like Velcro and positive statements slide off like Teflon. This means we all tend to walk around carrying the weight of everyone's criticisms on our backs. Not certain if this is true? Think of the most negative statement said to you as a child by your parent. Remember it? Now, think of the most positive. What is harder?

Children tend to remember negative statements said about them. Those who have negative behaviors tend to have even more negative criticisms heaped upon them by parents, peers, and even educators. So, if you are going to criticize, first start off with a positive comment about the situation and the students. Next, say the behaviorally specific thing you want to be changed and end with another positive comment and the child's strengths. In other words, the perceived negative information is neatly sandwiched with positive "breading" on either side (much like a sandwich).

NOTES

1. Richard Weissbourd, "Bullying Prevention: The Power of Empathy," *Huffington Post*, January 17, 2015, www.huffingtonpost.com/richard-weissbourd/bullying-prevention-the-power-of-empathy_b_6171238.html.

2. "Newton's Laws of Motion," Wikipedia, Wikimedia Foundation, March 27, 2018, en.wikipedia.org/wiki/Newton's_laws_of_motion.

3. Daniel Goleman, *Emotional Intelligence* (New York: Bantam Books, 1995).

4. "The Benjamin Franklin Effect: How to Build Rapport by Asking for Favors," Effectiviology, effectiviology.com/benjamin-franklin-effect/.

5. Ricki Linksman, "The Fine Line between ADHD and Kinesthetic Learners," Scribd, www.scribd.com/document/6706662/Misdiagnosed-ADHD.

6. Jensen, Christina Mohr, and Hans-Christoph Steinhausen, "Comorbid Mental Disorders in Children and Adolescents with Attention-Deficit/Hyperactivity Disorder in a Large Nationwide Study." ADHD Attention Deficit and Hyperactivity Disorder, Vol. 7, no. 1, 2014, pp. 27–38. doi: 10.1007/s12402-014-0142-1.

Conclusion

Don't just teach kids to count. Teach 'em what counts most.

—Karen Salmansohn

Please don't take this book merely as a toolbox of how to work with children who have behavioral issues. These are the youth who are drowning in a sea of emotion, situational discord, social skill, and/or neurological deficits.

They may have no one who is willing or able to reach their hand out and guide them through an ever-changing and frenetic world—a world that leaves them hurt, anxious, and confused. Many have no one to assure them that the nightmares that fog their child and adolescent years will eventually lift and show the rising sun of a new and hopeful tomorrow.

These students who reject and push you away, in seemingly the harshest tones, also need your care the most. Those who attack do so because they have not found a better way to swim in a life that is unpredictable and darkened with the constant storms of family and peer turmoil. They do so out of desperation and a lack of recognition of the spectrum of emotions that anger evokes.

Recognize that those who seemingly sit quietly on the fringes of school society may also be listening loudly to the screams of the voices within their own heads. These are voices of their self-loathing, criticism, and inward anger. These children equally need your care and mentoring.

Don't confuse lack of speaking for a lack of communication. Never forget or underestimate your amazing ability to sculpt our next generation.

It is far too easy to become jaded, to blame people and institutions, and to point fingers toward others and things that you cannot change (or change frustratingly slow at best).

Think continually of what is within your locus of control and it will expand. Constantly, step out of your locus of control and your abilities shrink and wither.

Consider your infinite possibilities of the former; it will bring you a rewarding career. Further, it shall foster a light for those countless children who will step through your school's doors and you will shine the glow for a new generation.

Appendix: Student School Climate Survey

1. Do you have at least one adult in school whom you can feel comfortable speaking with?

   a. Yes
   b. No

2. Do you feel safe in school most days?

   a. Yes
   b. No

3. Do you participate in at least one extracurricular activity after school (an activity that is school-sponsored but not during the regular school day)?

   a. Yes
   b. No

4. When you feel sad, angry, hopeless, or worried, whom are you most likely to talk to?

   a. I usually don't feel that way
   b. My mother or father
   c. Teacher or other adult in this school
   d. No one

5. How often do your parents ask about where you are or where you are going?

   a. Almost never
   b. Occasionally
   c. Half of the time
   d. Most of the time

6. Has your family ever discussed what they expect from you regarding potentially dangerous behaviors such as drinking alcohol, using drugs, or having sex?

   a. Yes
   b. No
   c. Sometimes
   d. Never

7. On a typical school day, how many hours do you watch TV, play video/computer games, or use technology for something that is not school-work? (Count time spent on things such as video game systems, an iPad or other tablet, a smartphone, texting, and social media.)

   a. I am not into technology or watching TV
   b. One to two hours a day
   c. Two to three hours a day
   d. More than three hours per day

8. In the last month, how often was there not enough food in your house?

   a. Always enough food
   b. Usually enough food
   c. Sometimes enough food
   d. Never enough food

9. Have you ever tried cigarette, alcohol, or drugs?

   a. Yes
   b. No

10. During the past year, did you ever feel so sad or hopeless almost every day for two weeks that you stopped doing some of your daily activities?

    a. Yes
    b. No

11. In the past thirty days, did you feel so bad about yourself that you thought about hurting or cutting yourself?

    a. Yes
    b. No

12. Have you ever been bullied at school, on the bus, or at school activities?

    a. Yes
    b. No

13. Have you ever been cyberbullied on your phone, social media, computer, or on video games?

    a. Yes
    b. No

14. Do you feel teachers and school administrators are aware of what goes on within the school?

    a. Usually
    b. Sometimes
    c. Rarely
    d. Never

15. Do you believe that this school is a good place for you to work and learn?

    a. Usually
    b. Sometimes
    c. Rarely
    d. Never

16. Do you think our school students and teachers respect and are kind to students and others who are different and diverse?

    a. Usually
    b. Sometimes
    c. Rarely
    d. Never

17. Do you believe teachers and students treat each other with respect and kindness?

    a. Usually
    b. Sometimes
    c. Rarely
    d. Never

18. Do you think when students don't follow rules, the consequences are fair and appropriate?

    a. Usually
    b. Sometimes
    c. Rarely
    d. Never

19. Do you think learning in school is interfered with because of other students' behaviors?

    a. Usually
    b. Sometimes
    c. Rarely
    d. Never

20. Do you enjoy school?

    a. Usually
    b. Sometimes
    c. Rarely
    d. Never

This is the end of the survey. Thank you!

Index

About the Author

Brett J. Novick holds a bachelor's degree in psychology from La Salle University in Philadelphia, Pennsylvania, and a master's degree in family therapy from Friends University in Wichita, Kansas, as well as postgraduate degree work and certification in school social work from Monmouth University in West Long Branch, New Jersey. Novick is licensed as a marriage and family therapist and state certified as a school social worker. He holds postgraduate certification as a supervisor, principal, and school administrator.

Novick has been working within school districts in New Jersey for the past fifteen years. In addition to his work as a school social worker/counselor, he has worked in private practice as well as a variety of community mental health settings, working with individuals, groups, and families. He also has experience working with children and families in crisis as an in-home therapist. Novick supervised a therapeutic children's shelter for youth in the care and custody of the state of Missouri as well and was employed as a coordinator of a county program in that state for families that had a member with a developmental disability.

He currently is an adjunct instructor at Rutgers University teaching postgraduate work in the subjects of dealing with difficult parents, behavioral issues with students, practical social skills for classified students, personality disorders, special education issues, and parental enrichment.

This is Novick's seventh book. His published books are *Parents and Teachers Working Together: Addressing School's Most Vital Stakeholders; The Likable, Effective, and Productive Educator: Being the Best You Can Be as an Educator; Don't Marry a Lemon!: A Marriage Therapist's advice on choosing the right mate the first time; Brain Bullies: Standing Up to Anxiety & Worry; Crappy to Happy: A Practical Guide for Finding Happiness; and The Balanced Child: Teaching Children and Students the Gifts of Social*

Skills. In addition, he has authored several national and international articles in education, educational administration, counseling, and social work.

In addition, Novick was awarded District Teacher of the Year in 2007–2008 and New Jersey School Counselors Association Human Rights Advocate of the Year in 2008. In addition, in 2011, he was honored with the New Jersey Council on Developmental Disabilities Inclusive Educator of the Year Award & Fellowship. He has received the New Jersey state governor's Jefferson Award for Public Service, the OCPGA Ocean County Counselor of the Year, the NJDOE Holocaust Education Commission's Hela Young Memorial, NJDOE Exemplary Educator, as well as the NJEA Dr. Martin Luther King Jr. Civil and Human Rights Awards, respectively.